Reclaiming Integration and the Language of Race in the "Post-Racial" Era

Reclaiming Integration and the Language of Race in the "Post-Racial" Era

Curtis Ivery and Joshua Bassett

ROWMAN & LITTLEFIELD
Lanham • Boulder • New York • London

Published by Rowman & Littlefield
A wholly owned subsidiary of The Rowman & Littlefield Publishing Group, Inc.
4501 Forbes Boulevard, Suite 200, Lanham, Maryland 20706
www.rowman.com

Unit A, Whitacre Mews, 26-34 Stannery Street, London SE11 4AB, United Kingdom

Copyright © 2015 by Rowman & Littlefield Publishers, Inc.

British Library Cataloguing in Publication Information Available

Library of Congress Cataloging-in-Publication Data

Library of Congress Cataloging-in-Publication Data Available
ISBN 978-1-4758-1518-4 (cloth : alk. paper) — ISBN 978-1-4758-1519-1 (pbk. : alk. paper) — ISBN 978-1-4758-1520-7 (electronic)

♾™ The paper used in this publication meets the minimum requirements of American National Standard for Information Sciences—Permanence of Paper for Printed Library Materials, ANSI/NISO Z39.48-1992.

Printed in the United States of America

Contents

Foreword

Eddie Glaude Jr.

In 1968, in response to the devastating violence in cities like Newark and Detroit, the Kerner Commission issued its report about the root causes of the riots and proposed dramatic steps to address the deep-seated problems plaguing the nation. For the members of the commission, America was "moving toward two societies, one black, one white—separate but unequal." The rebellions in America's cities demonstrated the inevitable imbrication of these two worlds: that whatever sense of powerlessness reigned in the nation's ghettos, those who lived there could precipitate chaos and bring down the curtain on this fragile experiment in democracy. Integration was not only a political imperative. It was a matter of life and death for the country.

The choices were clear. We could proceed with business as usual, "continuing both the proportion of the nation's resources now allocated to programs for the unemployed and the disadvantaged, and the inadequate and failing effort to achieve an integrated society." Or, the nation could embark on a bold and radical effort for full and genuine integration. For the members of the commission, "[o]nly a commitment to national action on an unprecedented scale [could] shape a future compatible with the historic ideals of American society." Such efforts required a radically different idea of who we took ourselves to be as Americans; it required "new attitudes, new understanding, and, above all, new will."[1]

What followed was a bold reimagining of the very fabric of this society. The commission proposed a major jobs initiative aimed at creating two million new employment opportunities—with one million in the public sector and a million in the private sector—"to absorb the hard core unemployed and materially reduce the level of underemployment for all workers, black and white."[2] They argued for an expansion of the federal social safety net, to protect the most vulnerable of Americans, and proposed a national system of income supplementation:

- To provide, for those who can work or who do work, any necessary supplements in such a way as to develop incentives for fuller employment;
- To provide, for those who cannot work and for mothers who decide to remain with their children, a minimum standard of decent living, and to aid in the saving of children from the prison of poverty that has held their parents.[3]

This proposed social safety net combined with critical recommendations around education and housing. In education, the proposals ranged from federal aid to school systems actively working to eliminate de facto segregation to robust early childhood education programs for every disadvantaged child in the country. In housing, the commission proposed programs "aimed at overcoming the prevailing patterns of racial segregation." The programs entailed a comprehensive federal open housing law and expansions of "the public housing program, with emphasis on small units on scattered sites and 'turnkey' programs."[4]

The rebellions in the country's cities, the commission argued, were not the result of some radical conspiracy or the ill-fated behavior of lawless people. The riots reflected, instead, a deep and abiding failure of the nation, one that we all too often refuse to see, to live up to its stated ideals. A radical transformation of the heart had to happen if the country was to move forward. And this wasn't empty moralist talk: the commission sought to account for the nation's ills in terms of the effects of interlocking experiences of marginalization, rooted in deep structural racial inequalities that distorted and disfigured American democracy. America had to put its money where its mouth was. As the report stated, "The major need is to generate new will—the will to tax ourselves to the extent necessary to meet the vital needs of the nation."[5]

Just twelve years later, with the election of Ronald Reagan to the presidency of the United States, America formally turned its back on the vision of the country proposed by the Kerner Commission. In fact, that vision was never fully embraced. From the beginning, reactionary forces challenged the pursuit of racial equality. Before the Kerner Commission report was released in 1968, the Civil Rights Act of 1966 failed to pass the U.S. Senate. That year, Republicans made significant gains in Congress as Democrats paid at the polls for their support of civil rights legislation. President Johnson even lamented, "the Negroes lost [the election]." When Ronald Reagan won the governor's seat in California, he said, without a hint of irony, that the election outcomes reflected the general sentiment that the country was moving "too fast." And, throughout the nation, white Americans expressed deep anxieties about the "lawlessness" of black political demonstrations. Calls for law and order set the stage for the mass incarceration of African Americans yet to come, and tax revolts in places. like California foreshadowed a national unwillingness to pay the costs for full racial equality and genuine integration.

In short, less than fifteen years after the passage of the Voting Rights Act in 1965, the country gave up on the honest pursuit of integration, declared itself color-blind, and placed the blame for persistent racial inequality squarely on the shoulders of those most burdened by its devastating effects.

For more than three decades now, Americans have been sold the idea that big government is bad and bloated bureaucracies are prone to corruption and that those who suffer on the margins of our society are there precisely because they have failed to show the kind of initiative requisite for success. We have also, ironically, bought into an idea expressed in the report of the 1975 Trilateral Commission, *The Crisis of Democracy*, in which they argued that the excesses of democracy stood in the way of governance: that the demands of racial egalitarianism and the expansion of democratic participation among the most vulnerable and marginal, in some ways, made democracies ungovernable.

Part of this transformation in the U.S. context involved abandoning any vision of integration on the scale of the Kerner Commission report and embracing fully the troublesome idea of disposable populations. As capitalism reorganized itself in the face of the massive disruptions of the "sixties," the ideology of neoliberalism took hold, which wasn't simply about economic policies predicated on facilitating free trade and dismantling the welfare state. Instead, as political theorist Wendy Brown argues, a powerful idea emerged as the logic of the market economy transformed the very conception of who we take ourselves to be and who we care about. We are now "rational, calculating creatures whose moral autonomy is measured by [our] capacity for 'self-care.'[6] On this view, race talk only blinds us to this fact and stands as an excuse for trading in victimization and avoiding accountability. The result is a citizenry with an anemic conception of the public good and blind to durable racial inequalities. Fellow-feeling dissipates as we relentlessly pursue whatever we imagine as success and the trope of color blindness fortifies our willful ignorance of those who languish in the shadows because, by the accident of birth, they were born poor and black.

Here the idea of genuine integration is tossed in the trash bin, for the idea suggests something more than the inclusion of black people into the fabric of American life. Genuine integration involves getting beyond racial fears, equalizing opportunity, and fundamentally transforming our national identity. All of which gets lost in the relentless pursuit of profit awash in an ethic predicated on competition and rivalry. In other words, we barely had a chance to pursue integration before the very framework for its bold enactment was dismantled by an attack on big government and the displacement of concerns of justice by the ideas of individual liberty and freedom in pursuit of selfish gain. What has been the result of this dramatic turn? To my mind and to the editors of this important volume, the answer is clear: America is no longer "moving toward two societies—separate and unequal." It has become one.

Reclaiming Integration and the Language of Race in the Post-Racial Era is a somber assessment of where we are as a nation and a powerful call, for those like-minded persons concerned about the future of this country, to take up the ethical demand for integration once again. America didn't just turn its back on the vision of integration offered by the Kerner Commission. Certain forces worked tirelessly to discredit the idea and to dismantle the gains of the black freedom struggle. So, we now live in a country as segregated as it was in the late 1960s. De jure segregation is no more. Jim Crow signs are relics of the past, artifacts in museums about southern history. But the fact remains, and it is a fact that indicts and convicts our fellow countrymen and women, residential segregation and segregation in public schools today approximate the levels of the late 1960s. New York State has the most segregated schools in the country and New York City, one of the most cosmopolitan cities in the world, has the most segregated schools in the state. This isn't a story of the legacy of southern racism. It is the outcome of the nation as a whole refusing to confront directly the reality of its failures. Or, worse still, the country has chosen to be exactly what it is: an oligarchy—a nation for the few.

Of course, matters have been complicated by the election of Barack Obama in 2008, the nation's first black president. Some pundits declared, and many Americans wanted to believe, that we had entered a post-racial era, a period in which race and racism no longer determined the life chances of any American citizen. But durable racial inequalities persist and the function of the discourse of post-racialism or color blindness is to effectively banish explicit talk of the effects of racial inequality in public debate. Race still matters. And aspirational claims for a time when it does not or efforts to ignore race altogether, as in the recent decisions of the Supreme Court, only exacerbate the current state of affairs.

The essays in this volume lay bare the insidious work of post-racial discourse and appeals to color blindness in blocking the way to full integration. The authors reveal how segregation affects the distribution of resources; short-circuits the life chances of particular groups; and, in the end, distorts democratic values. Underneath it all rests a host of entrenched beliefs and practices about black and brown people that we, as a nation, say we have left behind but in truth they still move us about. And here is the rub.

Genuine integration requires that we look the ugliness of who we are and who we have been squarely in the face. No shining city on the hill. No idea of

America as the Redeemer Nation or Americans as a chosen people. Instead, we must confront the fact that we have created a way of life predicated on the constant butchering of our most precious ideals. And that isn't an abstract formulation: it is evidenced in the black and brown children growing up in dire poverty, in the mass incarceration of black and brown men and women, in the chronic double-digit unemployment that plagues black communities, in the failure of public education, in the dramatic wealth gap between white and black Americans, and in the dashed dreams and darkening eyes of millions of our fellow Americans living in the shadows.

With this in mind, integration is not simply a political imperative. It is an ethical one. This powerful book makes this point crystal clear. Integration is not about a desire to be included into America as it is. It does not demand that those of us who have come up on "the other side of the tracks" give up the particular histories and experiences that make us who we are. Integration is not assimilation. It is a shorthand for the hard work of reimagining who we *all* are as Americans, of erasing racist boundaries that affect resource distribution, of eliminating prejudices and practices that cut off our fellows from the possibility of making real their dreams, and of finally getting rid of the idea that this is a white nation in the vein of old Europe.

The call to take up the demand for integration in a moment in which the language of color blindness dominates and the aspiration of getting beyond race reigns requires that we lay bare the truth: that we speak race when it matters and that we name racism for what it is. As long as white Americans believe that racial equality is a zero-sum game—that the more black folk gain the more white folk lose—we will never achieve our country. We need new attitudes, a radical imagination, and a new will to tackle the daunting task of genuine integration. It is a matter of life and death for this country and its creed. Liberty, Equality and Democracy are principles *and* practices, not mere words. To answer their promise, these editors have gathered some powerful thinkers who guide us toward how to achieve the elusive yet essential goal of integration.

NOTES

1. *Report of the National Advisory Commission on Civil Disorders* (New York: Bantam Books, 1968), 2, 22–23.

2. Ibid., 24.

3. Ibid., 27.

4. Ibid., 29.

5. Ibid., ix.

6. Wendy Brown, "Neo-liberalism and the End of Liberal Democracy," *Theory and Event* 7, no.1 (2003): 4–5.

Preface

Dr. Curtis L. Ivery

May 17, 1954, is a day I will never forget. There was a lot of pain on that day and a lot of happiness. The black community was elated because the U.S. Supreme Court had just declared segregated schools unconstitutional. This widely applauded ruling, known as *Brown v. Board of Education*, was going to change lives, instill hope, and carve out greater opportunities.

As a nine-year-old boy, I had only a marginal understanding of this, of course. I had no way of grasping the full magnitude of this decision and the impact it would have on society. And, yet, somehow, I got it. I got it when I saw elderly women crying and grown men dabbing their eyes. I got it when I heard the rousing speeches on the news.

Although I was too young to connect all of the dots, I had a vague and fuzzy understanding that education, as I knew it, was about to evolve into something bold and different. Looking back, it seems strange to me now. I had never sat next to a white student in class or competed against one in a chess match. I lived in a totally segregated world. How could I have possibly related to anything else? I was a fourth grader who should not have been able to recognize the inherent unfairness of racial separation or the significance of integration.

Yet, I did.

You see, I had already absorbed the notion that I was supposedly inferior. I knew that what had passed for education among my peers and me did not really measure up to the impressive academic offerings at segregated all-white schools. I also knew that I wasn't accepted there. So, I suppose it was with that awareness that I embraced the wonderful news that a black man named Oliver Brown had sued the school district and—with the help of attorneys, the NAACP, other litigants, and supporters—he had won.

He had succeeded in opening the government's eyes to the viability and nobility of educational institutions designed for everyone. More importantly, I would be included. My friends would be included.

Yes, I understood it, but only in a way that a fourth grader can. Secretly, I expected new friends, new teachers imparting new lessons and pushing us to pursue new dreams. But none of these things occurred. The ruling came and went and my classmates and I found ourselves at the same school, still reading the same tattered textbooks—the ones that were always passed on to us after the white students had finished using them. The names of those students, whom I perceived as more fortunate, were penned in the upper right hand on the first page of our hand-me-down books. Their names also managed to show up on certain school benches and were carved on the sides of our old, worn-out, wooden desks.

Three years later, my friends and I took it upon ourselves to put *Brown v. Board of Education* to the test. We decided to walk over to the local, all-white Catholic School and sign up. It was our lunch hour and we figured we could dash three miles and be back in time for our next class. So, dressed in our best, long pants and starched ties, we marched through the door, all smiles.

But we weren't smiling when we left. In our naiveté, we hadn't expected such a swift and blunt rejection. We didn't know who the gatekeeper was. Maybe he was the principal. Perhaps, he was the parish priest. All we knew is that a formidable male figure had made it clear that we were not wanted on the premises.

Experiences like that leave indelible impressions, especially on young minds. It was clear that we were still second and that change wouldn't be rearing its head any time soon.

When I think about our efforts then in the context of a nation still actively pursuing the aims and goals of integration to our current climate where integration no longer registers as a project of importance to far too many Americans, I can only return to widely voiced sentiments within civil rights communities that "our work is never done," that "the fight must always continue."

Such is the case with integration and racial equality. Our work here is not done. Our work here must continue.

The seeds of this project began approximately sixteen years ago when I moved to Detroit and began working on a series of educational and civil rights initiatives, including strongly advancing educational access to student populations, developing diversity programs in education, partnering with national entities to expand economic opportunities, and encouraging policy developments via numerous national conferences focusing on major issues of urban inequality.

Much of this critical work informs the thesis of this volume, which in its broadest terms focuses on two key areas: (1) what scholars have identified as the resegregation of U.S. schools to levels of racial segregation not seen since the 1960s, including what can be described as "new forms" of segregation in residential neighborhoods; and (2) the false, but widely believed idea, that America has become a "post-racial" society in which race and racial discrimination are said to no longer have impact on access to resources and opportunities in the United States.

This, of course, marks a stunning change from the civil rights era of the 1960s—and certainly earlier in 1954 from *Brown v. Board*—when the nation embarked upon its historic effort to integrate its public school systems from the inequality of segregation and similarly pursued policies that advanced economic opportunities for African American and Latino populations (and others) who had been denied such access on the basis of their race.

How this transformation occurred from integration and affirmative race-conscious policies to resegregation and a rejection of the idea that racial discrimination still has significant impact on our society is thus a critical question we must examine if we are to make any meaningful headway against the increasing, indeed, historic levels of economic inequality confronting our nation.

But there is also another significant area to address in this context as well, namely, examining how the nation is responding, on state and federal levels, to its unprecedented transformation into a multiracial majority, which is already occurring in our younger populations and will be achieved overall approximately in the next two decades.

The analysis offered here examines these various dynamics in a multidisciplinary framework, but our fundamental argument is that racial segregation and false ideas of racial equality as they continue to operate today pose a direct threat to our democracy and that we must therefore reclaim the project of integration as vital to our national interest. Moreover, to revitalize the project of integration in viable forms we must concurrently reclaim the language of race from the domain of post-racial discourse, which only exacerbates our increasing divisions by, again, denying their relevance. (Hence the title of this volume: *Reclaiming Integration and the Language of Race in the "Post-Racial" Era*.)

Despite the genuine progress we have made in race relations during the last half-century, and that has indeed been marked in significant ways by the election/reelection of President Obama, it can nonetheless be forcefully argued that we are trending backward in many important dimensions of race that if left unchecked will be detrimental to a nation on the cusp of historic multiracial transformation.

Acknowledgments

ACKNOWLEDGMENTS—CURTIS L. IVERY

Nothing means more to me in this world than my family. Therefore, it is a natural extension for me to be concerned about the state of our society, from our neighborhoods and local communities to the federal landscapes and global levels that touch our lives. And, I am. Not just for my family, but for all those with whom I share space in this world.

My professional life has been committed socially and educationally to the betterment of our communities; my personal life has been an extension of that commitment, working to impact and influence those individually and collectively for the greater good.

As we grow more technologically advanced, realize more visions and accomplishments as a society, we continue to wrangle with what sometimes seems to be the simplest of things: how to educate, engage, and employ those in urban communities; how to truly level the playing field and bridge the digital divide. And, while we have made progress, there remains much to do.

This book is an extension of my personal and professional commitment to make a difference; yet, this attempt to make a difference could not have been done without the support and participation of those who surround me.

My wife, Ola; my son, Marcus, and his family; and my daughter, Angela, and her family are the foundation upon which all I do proudly stands. I can't thank them enough for the love and joy they have given me, as well as the support they continue to extend in my efforts to touch and impact the lives of others.

I thank the generous contributions of all the exceptional scholars for their words and insight that are shared on these pages. It is an honor to share a commitment with others who I know care deeply for those in our communities.

And, I thank you for your willingness to engage this discussion and then share your thoughts and ideas with others for the collective good. We are indeed in this together, and only together will we truly ever make a difference.

ACKNOWLEDGMENTS—JOSHUA A. BASSETT

First and foremost I want to thank my friend and mentor Dr. Curtis L. Ivery, whose tireless work and vision for equality and social justice has been inspirational and never more essential than it is today in terms of the challenges confronting Detroit, the city to which we have devoted our professional lives.

I also wish to give my greatest thanks to the important work of the brilliant contributors to this volume who've dedicated their own lives in so many important ways to advancing our understanding, knowledge, and capacity to engage the critical issues of racial segregation and integration during this historic period of multiracial transformation in the United States. Special thanks here to Andrew Grant-Thomas and john powell, who've been amazing mentors and leaders.

Howard Winant's work (and Michael Omi's) has been nothing short of formative to the development of my critical scholarship: it's a dream come true to have had the opportunity to work with both these truly important scholars. Maria Krysan's work has been equally inspirational and I have been incredibly honored to have the opportunity to work with such an important scholar as well. And what can be said of Gary Orfield save to ask, is there any scholar working in the area of integration whose name comes up more often?

My thanks to Gary's close colleague Erica Frankenberg as well. And I also want to honor Robert Sedler's long and important legal work in civil rights.

My sincerest thanks to Stephen Kasser, who provided valued insights, and to Syreeta Tyrell, Darren Arquero, and Kaloma Cardwell for their support of our efforts.

All genuine love and gratitude to my family: my mom and dad, Leland and Tina; my twin brother, Robert, who's truly another version of me; my beautiful wife and mentor Michelle; and my eight-year-old son, Benicio, who I hope will one day read this . . . and be proud.

Chapter One

Introduction and Theoretical Overview

Curtis L. Ivery and Joshua A. Bassett

This book is the second of a two-volume set focusing on key issues related to the editors' civil rights work in Detroit and in a national context during the last fifteen years, including more than three decades of civil rights efforts conducted by Dr. Curtis L. Ivery, chancellor of Wayne County Community College District in Detroit and former commissioner of human services in Arkansas under then governor Bill Clinton.

In the first volume, titled *America's Urban Crisis and the Advent of Color-Blind Politics: Education, Incarceration, Segregation, and the Future of U.S. Multiracial Democracy* (Rowman & Littlefield, 2011), we drew upon our work in Detroit to analyze scholarship in the area of urban studies known widely as "urban underclass theory"[1] and called for the field to more directly engage the influence of so-called "race neutral," or "color-blind" politics,[2] in its analysis of the central causes of urban racial inequalities—in education, housing, employment, and other vital quality-of-life indices—that ignited the great civil rights movements of the 1950s/1960s and led to historic national reforms, including *Brown v. Board of Education*, the Civil Rights Act of 1964, the 1968 Fair Housing Act, and the implementation of affirmative action in economic and educational arenas.

This first book also called for analysis of color-blind politics to be applied to specific areas of education, mass incarceration, and segregation, and extend this work to the study of what scholars have only recently conceived as the concept/project of "multiracial democracy"[3] and why such a project is necessary for the future advancement of democratic institutions in the United States, especially given that "urban crisis"[4] conditions have arguably worsened during the last forty years[5] and remain crucial areas of social and civic concern.

1

In this second volume, *Reclaiming Integration and the Language of Race in the "Post-Racial" Era*, we move from a broad consideration of color-blind politics in sustaining racial inequalities, in terms of underclass "theory," to a focus on what we (and others[6]) consider to be the primary "structural" cause of enduring racial inequalities in the United States, namely, racial segregation and its continuing destructive impact on primarily African American, Latino, Asian[7] (and other nonwhite) populations' access to educational, economic, and political resources that are critical to the welfare of their communities. Our work here also moves from a context of color-blind politics, which have been identified as a driving force of conservative policies that emerged shortly after (and in opposition to) the adoption of major 1960s civil rights legislation,[8] to the more current context of the "post-racial" era (or "post-racial society"), wherein many political, institutional, and social groups advocate the entirely false, but widely held view,[9] that the United States, for all practical purposes, has achieved racial equality and thus racial identity and discrimination no longer exert any relevant influence in American life.[10]

Though often regarded as equivalent to color-blind discourse, post-racial rhetoric and the concept of the United States as a post-racial society, which many argue was achieved with the historic 2008 election of Barack Obama as the nation's first African American President,[11] actually represent a logical evolution of approximately four decades of preceding color-blind politics that, contrary to their thesis of advancing racial equality, have led to increased levels of racial inequality and segregation—even as the United States continues its accelerating transition into a majority multiracial society for the first time in its history.

In terms of segregation, the essays in this collection, all authored by leading scholars in their respective fields, focus on five key areas: (1) public education and what scholars have identified as the "resegregation" of U.S. schools to levels of racial segregation not seen since the mid-1960s;[12] (2) persistent and, what can be described as, "new forms" of racial segregation in residential housing that have emerged with the both the decline of white populations in the United States and the substantial increase of Latino, black, Asian, and multiracial populations;[13] (3) economic segregation and its direct links to racial segregation; (4) legal definitions of segregation as they apply to education and residential housing; (5) social concepts of segregation that have emerged in the advent of the post-racial era of U.S. race relations and their influence on broader ideas of integration as a means of achieving racial equality.

This multidisciplinary study of segregation (i.e., in education, sociology, law, economics, and language/cultural studies[14]) also operates as the framework for this volume's analysis of integration (i.e., within schools, housing, legal applications, social discourse) and similarly advances on traditional conceptions of integration as primarily a structural response to racial discrimination, usually within a black/white binary,[15] to a multiracial context that conceives of integration in new terminologies, including its role in the construction of social identity; its critical distinction from desegregation; its function in terms of the transition of the United States into a multiracial democracy; and, ultimately, its need to be reclaimed, on the same scale as *Brown v. Board*, as a project vital to our national interest.

We apply this theoretical approach because we believe as the nation approaches the last two decades of its unprecedented transformation into a multiracial majority, we must similarly conceive of a *new language of integration* appropriate to this evolution, one that will allow us to develop effective strategies to enduring patterns of segregation that if left unchecked will no doubt sustain current racial inequalities and, indeed, instantiate new racial hierarchies, or structures of racial stratification,[16] concurrent to the growth of nonwhite populations in the United States.

This effort to develop a new language of integration, we believe, necessarily requires that we also develop new models of "talking about race"[17]—or similarly, a *new language of race*—that are reflective of our transformative racial demographics and that vigorously interrogate the ascendance of class (i.e., class theories[18]) as a now dominant rationale in explaining social inequalities that would otherwise be identified as impelled by racial causes. The rise of class—and consequent minimization of race—as a dominant rationale of inequality has been identified by scholars[19] as a foundation of color-blind and related post-racial social views and is expanded here to what we argue is central to any efforts to reclaim the project of racial integration in the United States, namely, as the title of this collection indicates, that we must correlatively reclaim "the language of race," from the hegemony of post-racial discourse.

The project to reclaim racial integration, as a critical structure of democracy, can be related to a similar project advanced by Michael Omi and Howard Winant nearly thirty years ago in their now classic work, *Racial Formation in the United States*,[20] where they developed a new theory (i.e., "racial formation") that could provide a broad critical platform to understand the meaning and function of race in the United States. Among their many important analyses, Omi and Winant argue that a foundational cause of the nation's failures to adequately respond to racial inequalities is that we have no common language of race that allows us to effectively understand its influence as social and structural force in American society; no common vocabulary to even understand the concept of *racism*;[21] and thus no effective way to engage processes of racial discrimination and inequality, or the means that could allow us to negotiate past entrenched racial positions, or stagnant racial dialogues, that remain driving forces of division in the United States.

Our challenge to understand integration operates in similar terms. We lack a common vocabulary and language of racial integration, especially one that can apply to the workings of a multiracial society. We no longer have a national interest in pursuing integration as we did in the great civil rights eras of the 1950s and 1960s; no longer an imperative to advance integration in public education; no social or civic interest in encouraging integration in housing, as Douglass Massey and Nancy Denton have noted,[22] or expanding the scope of the 1968 Fair Housing Act; no longer a collective interest in integration in terms of voting rights, which have been dramatically reversed in just the last few years.[23] In sum, there are substantial majorities who no longer believe integration has relevance to our continuing evolution as a democracy, despite the fact, as noted, that racial inequalities in major quality-of-life indices (economics, education, health, etc.) continue unabated and race relations between blacks, whites, and Latinos during the last several years have been widely fractured: for example, in claims by conservatives that President Obama is "waging a war on whites";[24] via immigration policies (e.g., Arizona SB 1070; Alabama HB 56) that have the effect of criminalizing Latino identities; or the recent series of high-profile police killings of young black males, including unarmed teenager Michael Brown in Ferguson, Missouri, and twenty-two-year-old Darrien Hunt in Saratoga Springs, Utah, whose deaths have been decried by African American leaders as *prima facie* evidence of the persistent racism that continues to pervade majority white law enforcement of black communities.

Compounding the racial dynamics described above are the "on the ground" realities of segregation: in neighborhoods, schools, and urban and metro-suburban areas and the ways in which they will be shaped by increasing numbers of nonwhite populations and the effects this will have on access to existing and future educational and economic infrastructures. Moreover, these changing racial demographics raise important issues on what legal means can be availed by historically segregated communities to prevent their marginalization, both within consistently segregated, or more precisely, "hypersegregated"[25] areas, as well as in situations where processes of integration seem at work. Several essays in this volume address this very issue in their examination of important legal cases focusing on both segregation and integration, with some points of promise for equality, but overall it can be fairly stated that legal definitions (or thresholds) of racial segregation have succumbed to color-blind interpretations of constitutional law[26] and post-racial discourse that have rendered segregation very difficult to prove in legal terms, or at least in terms where structural legal remedies will be authorized by courts of law. A key premise of this legal transition (i.e., from explicit race-conscious policies that formed the architecture of major civil rights legislation of the 1950s/1960s to current color-blind legal approaches) is based on the fallacy that such civil rights legislation, over the course of decades, has been successful in eliminating segregation[27] on a governmental level and therefore unless segregation is manifest in overt, substantial, and state sponsored terms[28] then it is not legally relevant. This definition of what constitutes racial segregation has served as the basis for rejecting legal efforts to redress its sustaining disparate and negative impacts in education, housing, and affirmative action[29] and has strengthened, in our view, what we earlier identified as the ascendance of class-based rationale to explain inequalities that would otherwise be primarily located in racial origins. It has also, significantly, opened up class as a seminal site to develop and advance "race-neutral" policies, which scholars have shown are highly flawed[30] but that now dominate judicial approaches in addressing racial inequalities.

Reclaiming integration as a social and political structure of our democracy allows us to effectively respond to the major issues and conditions outlined here that continue to be driven by racial segregation. It directly provides a means to forward several imperatives:

- Implement a structural response to massive economic inequalities that continue to be oriented by race, where, on average, whites have twenty times the median wealth of blacks and eighteen times that of Latinos.[31]
- Reverse nearly three decades of continuous and increasing racial segregation in schools, which, as noted, have resegregated to levels not seen since the mid-1960s.[32]
- Dislocate the primacy of class-based rationale in social and legal arenas that continues to sustain racial inequalities and minimize the operations of structural racism in the United States.
- Reclaim the language of race from the domain of post-racial discourse, which effectively *deracinates* the relevance of race in social and political spheres and thereby adversely impacts race relations and drives racial divisions.
- Develop an infrastructure adequate to respond to the nation's expedient transition into a multiracial majority and correlative transformation into a multiracial democracy.[33]

THESIS AND CONTEXT

As noted, the multidisciplinary analysis of integration and segregation in this volume is drawn from five major areas: education, sociology, law, economics, and language/cultural studies. The purpose of this approach, among other identified interests, is to develop an overall critical framework of how racial segregation and discrimination continue to operate in specific areas of study within these respective fields and show their interdisciplinary relations. This is necessary, we argue, to offer as composite a view as possible of integration and its numerous functions in redressing racial inequalities and to examine how contemporary segregation operates in structural and discursive terms that must be accounted for in developing viable strategies of integration. The study of segregation as both an empirical social structure (e.g., in schools, neighborhood composition, political/economic institutions, etc.) and as a discourse (that is, in its simplest terms, as a language of representation[34]) reflects a long-standing model of analysis in the social sciences[35] (e.g., critical studies of race have utilized a structural/discursive methodology) that has gained renewed relevance in the context of our nation's multiracial transformation and advanced our understanding of segregation and integration in several key ways that inform the thesis of this collection, most notably in the recent theoretical work of Elizabeth Anderson and sociological studies of racial attitudes in housing conducted by Maria Krysan, Camille Zubrinsky Charles, Reynolds Farley, Lawrence Bobo, and noted others.

Anderson, specifically, in her book *The Imperative of Integration*, develops upon the seminal work of Charles Tilly to assert that racial segregation operates in two distinct but intersecting "modes" to produce inequalities: (1) "*spatial segregation*," which she defines as "processes that assign groups to different social spaces and institutions"; and (2) "*role segregation*," that is, "processes that assign groups to different social roles."[36] She extends her analysis of racial segregation via these dual modes, which have been applied in broader studies of "group inequality"[37] and share a common methodology with the structural/discursive model described above, to the examination of how segregation functions in two other interactive dimensions, namely, "stigmatization" and "discrimination."[38] Anderson's work here is important in that it advances, as with previous studies,[39] our conventional understanding of the concept of segregation as merely a structural process to one that produces the following effects:

1. Segregation produces racial stereotypes. This is a long-recognized process in critical studies of segregation[40] and is significant in understanding its social and psychological dimensions as well as, conversely, the ways in which *integration* can influence and construct social identities.[41]
2. Segregation produces racial stigmatization.[42] This stigmatization multiplies the effects of stereotypes on a group-wide level[43] in driving racial inequalities and, importantly, can marginalize groups in ways outside the

operations of explicit racial discrimination, such as via class or cultural stigmas.[44]

3. Segregation produces numerous types of discrimination—distinct from racial discrimination—in perpetuating racial inequalities.[45] These include "cognitive" and "evaluative" forms of discrimination,[46] which can result from implicit bias or apparently "non-prejudiced" social views.

4. Segregation—not discrimination—functions in its totality as the determinative cause of racial inequality in the United States; *"discrimination is a tool of segregation."*[47]

Anderson's analysis of the functions of segregation, stigmatization, and discrimination, which, again, outlines the rationale of the thesis of her work on integration, also addresses the ascendance of class dynamics in mitigating the function of race in perpetuating inequality[48] and can be related to influential sociological studies of race and class dynamics in housing choices, as noted, by Krysan, Farley, Bobo, Charles (et al.).[49]

Charles's and Bobo's work here is especially important in analyzing the operations of segregation and integration in residential housing beyond predominant binary studies[50] of black and white populations to a multiracial framework that includes the four major racial and ethnic groups in the United States: black, white, Latino,[51] and Asian. Their analysis of racial attitudes in housing choices is based on what is considered the most influential study of its kind to date, the 1992–1994 Multi-City Study of Urban Inequality (MCSUI),[52] which examined the causes of urban inequalities in the cities of Atlanta, Detroit, Boston, and Los Angeles and involved a group of nearly nine thousand respondents. Among their key findings is that while white racial attitudes on living in integrated areas has significantly improved since the 1970s, whites still lag substantially behind blacks, Latinos, and Asians in terms of levels of racial integration they will tolerate, and they are least comfortable of all racial groups in being a numerical minority.[53] Moreover, and of vital concern in understanding how dynamics of integration may develop with the increase of nonwhite populations, there is an emerging "racial hierarchy"[54] at work in housing choices wherein, according to Charles, "whites are always the most preferred out-group and blacks are unequivocally the least preferred."[55] This racial hierarchy, as it applies to whites, shows that whites prefer to live with Asians in notable majorities higher than Latinos and least of all blacks[56] and represents what we believe is an important example of the distinct effects of racial stigmatization on racial groups. We further argue that any viable efforts to limit segregation and encourage integration must account for the various operations of this emerging racial hierarchy.

Krysan's (Farley et al.) highly innovative video experiment/study[57] of racial preferences in housing also informs the analysis of this collection via its examination of race and class dynamics in segregation. As noted, class discourse in its various formations (social, legal, ethnocentric, etc.)[58] has emerged as a dominant rationale in explaining inequalities that would otherwise appear to be directly linked to racial causes, but Krysan's video study of neighborhood choice provides empirical evidence that race significantly operates in ways independent of class. In this study, survey participants were shown and asked to evaluate a video series of actual neighborhoods in Chicago and Detroit that were identical except in terms of the race of the residents (hired actors) walking through the neighborhoods, so that the same neighborhood on video appeared with all blacks in one segment, all whites in another, and also with a mixed racial composition. Despite the fact that the neighborhoods were visually identical—which according to class-based rationale should have rendered these neighborhoods equivalent to respondents—a racial hierarchy emerged in their evaluation where whites assessed the all-white neighborhoods as better than the racially mixed and the all-black neighborhoods as the least desirable (a pattern that, Krysan notes, has been confirmed in other survey studies[59]). For blacks, this survey data showed that racial composition of the neighborhoods mattered significantly less than it did for whites in total (affirming Charles's work) and that both the all-black and racially mixed neighborhoods were preferable to all-white neighborhoods.

The critical work of Krysan, Farley, Bobo, Charles, and Anderson outlined above offers important theoretical, analytical, and empirical perspectives to understand contemporary operations of segregation and integration in the United States and more specifically, as noted, directly applies to the multiracial and multidisciplinary critical framework that informs the thesis of this collection. We will provide a more detailed synopsis of this work within these respective disciplines at the close of this section, but would now turn our discussion toward the other major area of analysis of our work, which focuses on the function of language in relation to race and integration.

Language, Race, and Integration

In their insightful analysis on the status and legacy of *Brown v. Board* on its sixtieth anniversary, Gary Orfield and Erica Frankenberg (et al.) of the influential Civil Rights Project at UCLA/Proyecto Derechos Civiles report that in terms of legal and governmental decisions/actions supporting integration and race relations initiatives there have been no meaningful actions since the early 1970s, with "the last major Supreme Court [SCOTUS] decision expanding desegregation policies . . . in 1973 [and] the last major Congressional action[s]" occurring in 1972.[60] Orfield and Frankenberg further report that since 1974, starting with the crucial *Milliken v. Bradley* decision, which effectively nullified inter-district school desegregation,[61] SCOTUS decisions have had limited capacities to desegregate schools and actually terminated "desegregation plans and [prohibited] major forms of voluntary desegregation [from] 1991–2007."[62]

This four-decade body of law provides a critical historical template to analyze the architecture of legal theory that limited and eventually dismantled integration from *Brown* in a broad spectrum of areas, including legal definitions of segregation, governmental requirements of desegregation, the transition from race- to class-based remedies in redressing racial inequality and, ultimately, current terminologies of the use of race in student assignment that have actually equated the functions of integration and segregation in constitutional law. This conflation of integration and segregation was specifically determined in the 2007 SCOTUS case, *"Parents Involved in Community Schools,"* ("PICS"),[63] which banned voluntary integration programs in Seattle and Kentucky school districts on what many consider the disturbing legal premise that using race as a factor to achieve integration in schools is legally indistinguishable from using race as a factor to achieve segregation. Justice Roberts's and Thomas's opinions on this matter are clear: "What do the racial classifications do in these cases, if not determine admission to a public school on a racial basis? Before *Brown*, schoolchildren were told where they could or could not go to school based on the color of their skin. The school districts in these cases have not carried the heavy burden of demonstrating that we should allow this again" (Roberts, Section IV).[64] And Thomas, affirming this equivalence, "[A]ll race based government decisionmaking [sic]—regardless of context—is unconstitutional. . . . What was wrong in 1954 cannot be right today."[65]

Again, the legal decisions concerning desegregation during the last forty years are critical to analyzing how the language of law evolved to define the legal terms and conditions that eventually dismantled integration in U.S. schools, but we would also extend this analysis from a legal context to a social, or more precisely, semiotic context,[66] in order to argue that language also functions in these cases to construct concepts of integration in terms of social identity, primarily in nationalist, color-blind, and post-racial "frames,"[67] or paradigms. The 1979 U.S. District Court case, *Armour v. Nix*[68] offers a potent example here. This case, a class action suit filed by "black indigent parents" against county, city, and sate school boards of Atlanta for an "interdistrict remedy to yield a truly integrated school situation," is premised on the argument that historical practices of legal segregation in schools and housing—notwithstanding the passage of civil rights laws prohibiting such actions—have enduring effects that continue to produce racial inequalities in schools and should thus be subject to integrative remedy. The court dismissed the parents' actions on the legal position/precedent that because "present day governmental actions in no way contributed to residential [and school] segregation" that there was no basis to "justify judicial intervention."[69]

This position of the government's legal responsibility (or lack of) for segregation is consistent to the present day, but what is striking about *Armour* is how language is used to describe integration as something potentially *dangerous* to society—that is, as the "imposition of a drastic . . . remedy" that if applied to the area of residential segregation would no less than "rip up the very fabric of society."[70]

This description of integration as a potentially "drastic" force with the capacity to "rip up the very fabric of society" has strong nationalist connotations that stigmatize integration (and by extension, its proponents) as somehow antisocial, antidemocratic, and consequently anti-American, which is in direct opposition to its historical function (via *Brown*) as an essential component of American democracy. It also redefines integration, as stated, in terms that can be related to scholarship focusing on color-blind and post-racial frames of racism and progressive race-conscious discourse. A noted example of the former is developed in the work of Eduardo Bonilla-Silva and his conception of the "central frames of color-blind racism,"[71] where he argues that integration, affirmative action, and related race conscious policies that were initially developed to redress racial inequalities have been recast from potential democratic interventions to those that now threaten "American individualism . . . liberalism . . . 'equal opportunity' . . ." and American identity itself.[72] Leading civil rights law professor john powell (uses no caps) and critical race scholar Andrew Grant-Thomas have also identified this similar process in regard to social constructions and dialogues of race, particularly in their several years of work as director/codirector of the Kirwan Institute for the Study of Race and Ethnicity and its national "Transforming Race" conferences (2007–2010) that focused on developing effective race-conscious language, dialogues, and policies that could be mobilized to respond to racial inequalities sustained by color-blind and post-racial sociopolitical dynamics.

The study of integration and race in terms of language in the legal and social science spheres outlined above offers a significant critical approach to analyze key structures of segregation and inequality that we propose (per our earlier discussion) can be advanced by linking such efforts to formal studies of representation and race, specifically those grounded in semiotic theory as in the influential work of Stuart Hall and his colleagues at the Open University.[73] Hall's work is especially relevant to studies of integration as a language, specifically in its analysis of racial stereotypes as a set of representational practices that naturalize inequality through "essentialist" (i.e., biological) views of race and culture (e.g., ideas that races naturally prefer to live with their own kind; the use of culture to explain why blacks and Latinos lag behind whites in educational outcomes, etc.)[74] and operate within what he defines as a "racialized regime of representation,"[75] which he outlines in a historical framework of segregation and integration and that we believe can be a useful model to understand how stereotypes function to produce racial hierarchies. Given, again, that scholars have developed a persuasive body of work demonstrating that racial segregation produces stereotypes, Hall's work can provide valuable insight as to how stereotypes stigmatize racial identity as well as a template to develop strategies, what Hall defines as "trans-coding" strategies,[76] to counter such effects.

Chapter Organization

As noted, this collection is a multidisciplinary study of segregation and integration organized in five major areas of study: education, sociology, law, economics, and language/cultural studies.

We've attempted to frame this critical work as it applies to two projects (as identified by the title of this book) that we argue are essential to advancing the principles of American democracy (i.e., multiracial democracy) as the U.S. undergoes its historic transformation into a majority multiracial society. These projects are: (1) reclaiming integration; and (2) reclaiming the language of race. We have argued here that both projects are necessarily interrelated and can only be effective if considered in the context of color-blind politics and the advent of the post-racial era of U.S. race relations, which, with the two historic elections of President Obama, have been identified as forming a now dominant paradigm of racial discourse in American society.[77] The following synopses organize the chapters comprising this collection within this framework and outline a critical context to the designated areas of study. (Note that several chapters can be applied to multiple areas of study.)

Education: Essays by Gary Orfield, Erica Frankenberg, Eddie Glaude Jr., and john powell provide a broad scope of analysis of integration and segregation in terms of educational practices, policies, legislative/judicial reforms, and the role of integration in improving educational outcomes, racial inequalities, and foundational structures of American democracy. Orfield and Frankenberg's work focuses on major court rulings dealing with affirmative action and integration (and similarly apply to the area of "law" cited here), while Glaude's and powell's respective analyses examine integration in political dimensions, economics, and the construction of social identity. Related critical issues here include: the resegregation of American schools to levels of racial segregation not seen since the 1960s; the abandonment of educational polices/practices dealing with integration and race since the 1970s/80s (respectively); the historic transformation, in 2014, of the student population of U.S. public schools into a multiracial majority;[78] the rise of Latinos as the largest student populations in the South and Western United States; and the significant conditions of economic inequality among racial groups in education, wherein blacks and Latinos attend schools with almost twice as many low-income students as whites or Asian populations.

Sociology: Essays by Maria Krysan, Howard Winant, and Andrew Grant-Thomas focus on various sociological areas of race, integration, and segregation, including color-blind racial attitudes in housing; race as structuralizing force of U.S. social and economic order; and the role of implicit bias in driving racial and social attitudes. Krysan's work importantly examines the intersecting functions of race and class in housing choices to expose how racial attitudes, counter to class dynamics, play a determinative role in residential segregation. Winant's analysis outlines the concept of a "racial regime" and its function in sustaining racial inequality and segregation; while Grant-Thomas's analysis (which also applies to the area of "language") examines the operations of implicit bias in various areas of racial discourse and identity. Critical issues here include: the emergence of a racial hierarchy in residential housing choices; the effects of segregation in producing stereotypes; and the recognition (as in powell's and Glaude's work and related scholarship) that integration can operate beyond structural terms of desegregation to construct social identity.

Law: Robert Sedler, lead attorney of the historic early 1970s Louisville, Kentucky, desegregation case, which was one of a few rare cases successful in implementing inter-district school integration post *Milliken v. Bradley*,[79] but overturned in the 2007 SCOTUS *PICS* decision (as earlier noted), offers a sobering overview of the current state of integration in U.S. public schools and the various legal and institutional means employed post *Brown* that have revitalized levels of racial segregation to that of the 1960s. Sedler points to the implementation of geographic school attendance zones, narrowing legal definitions of segregation, and social practices of whites in removing their kids from public schools as driving forces of racial resegregation, for which currently there are few, if any, viable solutions. Orfield, Frankenberg, and powell (as noted) also discuss key legal cases analyzing the devolution of integration in public schools and higher education, including analysis of the Louisville, Kentucky, school district in the aftermath of the *PICS* decision, which may yet provide a template to revive integration on broader scales. Critical issues here include: the mitigation and shift from race-conscious to class-conscious policies in redressing racial segregation and inequality; potential increasing restrictions on affirmative action in higher education (and related areas); potential challenges to the long-standing legal precedent that there is a "compelling interest" to racial diversity in education.

Economics: Reynolds Farley, Lucie Kalousova, and Sheldon Danziger analyze racial disparities in economics in their respective essays focusing on Detroit and its neighboring suburbs both historically and in the aftermath of the "Great Recession" of 2007–2009 in the U.S., where continuing through 2011 approximately one-quarter of U.S. households lost at least 75 percent of their net worth, with median wealth falling a staggering 53 percent for blacks compared to 16 percent for whites (between 2005 and 2009).[80] Their work shows a strong correlation between what can be described as economic segregation and racial segregation and applies a substantial set of original and established economic metrics that examine poverty and racial economic inequality in multiple domains, including housing, unemployment, financial insecurity, education, gender, and other areas, with Farley's work extending much of this analysis to a national level. Kalousova and Danziger outline various public policies that can be adopted to encourage "the racial economic integration of Detroit," which could also be applied nationally, and Farley's work offers a sweeping overview of the evolution of racial, governmental, and economic forces that drove Detroit, once the nation's fourth-most-populated city, into its historic bankruptcy (the largest of its kind in U.S. history). Related critical issues here include: analyses of how blacks and Latinos experience poverty in ways that are much more severe than white and Asian populations, with low-income whites (on average) residing in neighborhoods where one in ten residents are poor, while blacks and Latinos live in areas with much higher rates of concentrated poverty;[81] the effects of racial segregation in producing generational poverty for blacks and Latinos, in contrast to whites, whose experience of poverty is far less sustained;[82] and emerging work by scholars such as Richard Kahlenberg focusing on "the economic integration movement."[83]

Cultural Studies/Language: We have outlined what we argue are major areas of study of the relationship between integration, race, and language (i.e., a historical analysis of legal vocabularies of segregation and integration; the ascendance of color-blind and post-racial frames of racial identity; semiotic analyses of race, representation, and stereotypes) with several of our contributors—powell, Winant, Krysan, Glaude, Grant-Thomas—providing work that can be directly applied to these areas, but we would refer to a key point in powell's essay where he writes the following in outlining the geography of integration, language, and social identity: "Integration . . . is not just material . . . It is a project with ontological implications . . . [It] is not just about the separation and distribution of material goods or geographic space, but the constitution and distribution of *being*" (emphasis added). This concept of integration as a "constitution of being" is directly relevant to a central thesis of cultural studies, wherein language is analyzed far beyond its most general dimensions as a form of writing or speech to its function, as famously conceived by Michel Foucault, as a *discourse* that constructs social identity.[84] This, in our view, is a critical aspect to reclaiming the project of racial integration in our educational systems, neighborhoods, and, by extension, our body politic. Our very identity as a democracy depends upon it.

CONTEXT: DETROIT

As this book goes to press, we would be remiss in not locating its critical analysis in the so-called "real-world" context of Detroit, a city where we have collectively worked on issues of racial equity for some three decades and which is now emerging from bankruptcy to confront what is certainly a difficult future, especially as it directly affects our substantial black and lower-income populations who, despite some recently promising areas of revitalization (primarily in downtown Detroit), remain almost locked in vast swaths of neighborhoods that offer only the most minimal access to educational and economic resources that are essential to their recovery. These very conditions have endured for more than sixty years and reflect why Detroit is one of the most important cities in the United States to analyze how racial segregation operates in multiple structural frameworks to produce inequalities. Detroit's history in this context has been brilliantly studied by such works as Thomas Sugrue's classic text, *The Origins of the Urban Crisis*, and Farley, Danziger, and Harry Holzer's important book, *Detroit Divided*, which have analyzed the political, economic, and social forces that caused this segregation and ultimately led to Detroit's unprecedented racial transformation in a mere decade from a majority white population in 1970—(815,823 whites; 659,022 blacks)—to majority black population in 1980 (754,274 blacks; 402,077 whites).[85] This includes analysis by Sugrue, for example, of how the construction of the nation's first freeway systems in Detroit destroyed black neighborhoods and functioned as physical barriers of racial segregation,[86] or Farley's assessment of unique legislative policies that isolated Detroit from its surrounding areas with scarce incentives for cooperation. As Farley notes: "Detroit is surrounded by 158 other separate and distinct municipalities . . . with few, if any, incentive to cooperate. . . . [It] differs from every other major city on most every important dimension . . . and is different because of the way racial polarization occurred within an ineffective system of local government."[87]

To be sure (as Farley, Sugrue, and others identify), there are other causes of Detroit's decline that do not directly involve race—economic deindustrialization, inadequate government, a lack of diverse work industries—but in our view, racial dynamics, and specifically racial segregation, remain the major factors that must be addressed if the city is to make any viable headway against the cyclical forces of urban inequality that have driven it to its current economic state, its perilous situation with significant numbers of residents confronting potential neighborhood relocation and water shut-offs,[88] and the meteoric decline of its white populations who, as noted, numbered more than 800,000 in 1970, but accounted for approximately 75,000 in 2010.[89]

Lastly, and in the context of the major thesis of this collection, as Detroit proceeds with its plans for recovery in its post-bankruptcy, and, again, we note there is some cause for optimism, especially in terms of the influx of recent financial capital and integrative dynamics occurring in the city's downtown and neighboring areas, we fully believe that any sustainable revitalization will not be possible without the racial integration of Detroit's public schools, which remain overwhelmingly racially segregated and, so far, without viable institutional support and resources to effectively pursue integration.

NOTES

1. Thomas J. Sugrue outlines three major areas of "urban underclass" theory in his influential book *The Origins of the Urban Crisis* (Princeton, NJ: Princeton University Press, 1986), 4–11.

2. See Maria Krysan's significant work, "From Color Caste to Color Blind, Part I: Racial Attitudes in the U.S. during World War II, 1935–1945"; "Part II: Racial Attitudes during the Civil Rights and Black Power Eras, 1946–1975"; and "Part III: Contemporary Era Racial Attitudes, 1976–2004," in *The Oxford Handbook of African American Citizenship 1865—Present*, Henry Louis Gates, Jr., et al., eds. (Oxford: University Press, 2012), 178–235.

3. For a critical overview of the concept of multiracial democracy see Curtis L. Ivery and Joshua A. Bassett, eds., *America's Urban Crisis and the Advent of Color-Blind Politics: Education, Incarceration, Segregation and the Future of U.S. Multiracial Democracy* (Lanham, MD: Rowman & Littlefield, 2011), 133–61.

4. See Sugrue, *The Origins of the Urban Crisis*, 1–14.

5. See, for example, Edward W. Brooke, former senator and member of the historic Kerner Commission, "King and Kerner: An Unfinished Agenda," *Washington Post*, April 3, 2008, A-17.

6. See Xavier de Souza Briggs's edited collection, *The Geography of Opportunity: Race and Housing Choice in Metropolitan America* (Washington, DC: Brookings Institution Press, 2005). Also, Elizabeth Anderson, *The Imperative of Integration* (Princeton, NJ: Princeton University Press, 2010), 63–66.

7. Brandon Yoo offers a broad overview of studies concerning the "model minority myth" of Asian Americans in his online article, "Unraveling the Model Minority Myth of Asian American Students," *Education.com*, October 25, 2010, retrieved from http://www.education.com/reference/article/unraveling-minority-myth-asian-students/.

8. Eduardo Bonilla-Silva, *Racism without Racists* (Lanham, MD: Rowman & Littlefield, 2006), 1–24.

9. See Ivery and Bassett, *America's Urban Crisis and the Advent of Color-Blind Politics*, 21–51, where we provide an overview of this scholarship.

10. See Bonilla-Silva, *Racism without Racists*, 25–52.

11. The *Wall Street Journal*, for example, noted that after his first election in 2008, "President Elect Obama . . . ha[d] a special obligation to . . . put to rest the myth of racism as a barrier to achievement in [the United States.]," November 5, 2008, A-22.

12. Gary Orfield, John Kucesar, and Genevieve Siegel-Hawley, *E Pluribus . . . Separation: Deepening Double Segregation for More Students* (Los Angeles: UCLA/Civil Rights Project/Proyecto Derechos Civiles, 2012), xviii.

13. U.S. Census Bureau, "U.S. Census Bureau Projections Show a Slower Growing, Older, More Diverse Nation a Half Century from Now," retrieved December 12, 2012 from http://www.census.gov.

14. Stuart Hall provides important insight here on the critical study of language and the construction of racial identity in *Representation: Cultural Representations and Signifying Practices* (London: Sage, 1997), 225–90.

15. See Camille Zubrinsky Charles, "Can We Live Together? Racial Preferences and Neighborhood Outcomes," in *The Geography of Opportunity: Race and Housing Choice in Metropolitan America*, ed. Xavier de Souza Briggs (Washington, DC: Brookings Institution Press, 2005), 52. Bonilla-Silva, *Racism without Racists*, 177–205.

16. Bonilla-Silva, *Racism without Racists*, 177–205.

17. We refer here to significant work by john powell, Andrew Grant-Thomas, et al., via their national "Talking about Race" conferences and related scholarship for the Kirwan Institute for the Study of Race and Ethnicity (The Ohio State University), 2007–2010.

18. Michael Omi and Howard Winant provide an incisive analysis of class in this context in *Racial Formation in the United States* (New York: Routledge, 2015), 53–73.

19. Ibid.

20. Ibid.

21. As Omi and Winant note: "Until we understand the concept of race, it is impossible effectively to analyze the familiar issues which involve race . . . to grasp the way racial identity is assigned and assumed . . . to recognize the enduring role race plays in . . . organizing social inequalities . . . [and] shaping the very geography of American life," *Racial Formation in the United States* (New York: Routledge, 1994 edition), vii.

22. Douglass Massey and Nancy Denton, *American Apartheid: Segregation and the Making of the Underclass* (Cambridge, MA: Harvard University Press, 1994), 4.

23. See, for example, Ryan J. Reilly, Mike Sacks, and Sabrina Saddiqui, "Voting Rights Act Section 4 Struck Down by Supreme Court," *Huffington Post*, June 6, 2013, http://www.huffingtonpost.com/2013/06/25/voting-rights-act-supreme-court_n_3429810.html.

24. Erica Werner, "Rep. Brooks Charges War on Whites by Democrats," Associated Press, August 6, 2014.

25. Massey and Denton, *American Apartheid*, 74–78.

26. See, for example, Jeffery Rosen, "The Color Blind Court," *American University Law Review* 45 (1996): 791.

27. Bonilla-Silva, *Racism without Racists*.

28. See, for example, the 1979 legal case *Armour v. Nix*: "Before . . . school districts may be set aside . . . for remedial purposes or by imposing a cross-district remedy, it must . . . be shown that racially discriminatory acts of the state or local school districts . . . have been a substantial cause of interdistrict segregation. The requirement that there be a constitutional violation contemplates a substantial violation. Neither a de minimis violation nor a cumulative violation will justify an interdistrict remedy," 1979 U.S. Dist. Lexis 9609, p. 2.

29. See, for example, Richard Lempert and William Kidder, "State Should Clarify Argument in Affirmative Action Case," *Detroit Free Press* (online edition), November 4, 2013.

30. Nikole Hannah-Jones provides a fine summary here in "Class Action: A Challenge to the Idea That Income Can Integrate America's Campuses," *ProPublica*, June 24, 2013, retrieved from http://www.propublica.org/article/class-action-a-challenge-to-the-idea-that-income-can-integrate-americas-cam.

31. Rakesh Kochhar, Richard Fry, Paul Taylor, "Wealth Gaps Rise to Record Highs between Whites, Blacks, Hispanics," Pew Research Center, July 26, 2011, retrieved from http://www.pewsocialtrends.org.

32. Orfield, Kucesar, and Siegel-Hawley, *E Pluribus . . . Separation*.

33. Ivery and Bassett, *America's Urban Crisis and the Advent of Color-Blind Politics*.

34. Hall, *Representation*.

35. As Omi and Winant argue: "From a racial formation perspective, race is a matter of both social structure and cultural representation. Too often, the attempt is made to understand race simply or primarily in terms of only one of these two analytical dimensions," *Racial Formation in the United States* (1994), 56.

36. Anderson, *The Imperative of Integration*, 9.

37. See, for example, Mary R. Jackman, *The Velvet Glove: Paternalism and Conflict in Gender, Class, and Race Relations* (Berkeley: University of California Press, 1994), 128–38.

38. Anderson, *The Imperative of Integration*, 44.

39. See, for example, Maria Krysan, "Whites Who Say They'd Flee: Who Are They, And Why Would They Leave?" *Demography* 39, no. 4 (November 2002): 675–96.

40. Ibid.

41. Anderson, *The Imperative of Integration*, 44.

42. Ibid., 65.
43. Ibid., 48.
44. Ibid., 57–60; 70–73.
45. Ibid., 65–66.
46. Ibid., 57–60.
47. Ibid., 64.
48. Ibid., 70–73.
49. Ibid.
50. Charles, "Can We Live Together?"
51. Latino, or Hispanic, is still considered an ethnic category, but there are currently many well-documented and active debates to change this terminology to a racial category.
52. Charles, "Can We Live Together?," 52–53.
53. Ibid., 45–63.
54. Ibid.
55. Ibid.
56. Ibid.
57. Maria Krysan, Mick P. Couper, Reynolds Farley, and Tyrone Forman, "Does Race Matter in Neighborhood Preferences? Results from a Video Experiment," *NIHMSID* 115, no. 2 (September 2009): 527–59.
58. See Anderson, *The Imperative of Integration*, for example, 69–73.
59. Krysan's citation is in her essay for this volume, chapter 2,"Are We Colorblind? A View from the Neighborhood."
60. Orfield, Frankenberg, with Jongyeon Ee and John Kuscera, *Brown at 60: Great Progress, a Long Retreat and an Uncertain Future* (Los Angeles: UCLA/Civil Rights Project/Proyecto Derechos Civiles, May 15, 2014), 4.
61. Robert Sedler offers an important analysis here in "The Profound Impact of *Milliken v. Bradley*," *Wayne Law Review* 33, no. 5 (1986–1987): 1693.
62. Orfield et al., *Brown at 60*, 4.
63. *Parents Involved in Community Schools v. Seattle School District No. 1*, 551 U.S. 701 (2007).
64. Ibid., section IV.
65. Ibid., Thomas, 6, 33.
66. Hall, *Representation*, 36–51.
67. Tom Rudd, john powell, Andrew Grant-Thomas, et al. provide an excellent summary of the critical concept of "framing" in *Talking about Race: Resource Notebook* (Columbus: Kirwan Institute for the Study of Race and Ethnicity, The Ohio State University, 2009).
68. *Armour v. Nix*, 1979 U.S. Dist. Lexis 9609.
69. Ibid., 2.
70. Ibid., 11–12.
71. Bonilla-Silva, *Racism without Racists*, 25–52.
72. Ibid.
73. Hall, *Representation*.
74. Charles, "Can We Live Together?"

75. Hall, *Representation*, 257–74.

76. Ibid., 270.

77. Bonilla-Silva, *Racism without Racists*.

78. Kimberly Hefling, and Jesse J. Holland, "White Students No Longer to Be Majority in School," Associated Press, August 10, 2014.

79. Charles, "Can We Live Together?".

80. See Lucie Kalousova and Sheldon Danziger's essay in this volume, "Disparities in Economic Well-Being in the Detroit Metropolitan Area after the Great Recession."

81. Hannah-Jones, "Class Action."

82. See, for example, Richard Rothstein, "The Urban Poor Shall Inherit Poverty," *American Prospect*, January 7, 2014, retrieved from https://prospect.org/article/urban-poor-shall-inherit-poverty.

83. Hannah-Jones, "Class Action."

84. Hall, *Representation*, 41–51.

85. The *Detroit News* and U.S. Census Bureau statistics.

86. Sugrue, *The Origins of the Urban Crisis*, 47–51.

87. See Reynolds Farley's essay in this volume, "The Future of Detroit: How the City Got to Where It Is Now and What Is Next."

88. "Groups Discuss Detroit Water Shutoffs with UN Experts," Associated Press, October 19, 2014.

89. Quoted in Ross Eisenberry, "Detroit's Bankruptcy Reflects a History of Racism," *Working Economics*, Economic Policy Institute blog, February 25, 2014, http://www.epi.org/blog/detroits-bankruptcy-reflects-history-racism/.

Chapter Two

Are We Color-Blind?

A View from the Neighborhood

Maria Krysan

The observation that durable racial inequalities define our country is supported by studies demonstrating racial/ethnic differences in income, education, wealth, occupation, health, school quality, political influence, and the list goes on. Taken together, this evidence belies the assertion that America is "post-racial" or that its citizens are "color-blind." The purpose of my chapter is not to demonstrate or document that these structural racial inequalities continue to pervade American society (I leave this to other chapters in the volume) but instead to examine the evidence about one of the supporting actors in this structural system of inequality: the racial attitudes held by individuals that, together, constitute the ideological and discursive framework in which one dimension of race relations in the United States is played out. To preview the conclusion: attitudes have changed; but race still matters.

To support this observation, I use the arena of housing as something of a case study because it offers macro-level, meso-level (or mid-level), and micro-level data to shed light upon, and illustrate, the continued manifestation of racial inequality. Moreover, because so much of what happens to people in their life depends on where they live, it has been argued that racial residential segregation—the fact that people of different races and ethnicities generally do not share the same neighborhoods—is the structural linchpin of racial inequality in America (Bobo 1989; Pettigrew 1979). One needs to look no further than the area of life at the core of this volume—schools—to understand the importance of housing in shaping substantially unequal opportunities. If we are in fact color-blind, for example, then the racial composition of a neighborhood should not matter in regard to whether one finds it desirable. If we are color-blind, it should not matter to us what our neighbors' race/ethnicity is. If we are color-blind, it should not matter if we are white, black, Latino, or Asian, when we approach a real estate agent or landlord to inquire about a place to live. Although my interest ultimately is in the structural inequality reflected in housing, my focus in this essay is on the micro-level processes, as reflected in the attitudes, beliefs, and perceptions that undergird this and other structures. The argument is not that these are more or less important than other forces at play. Rather, they are one part of the complex web of factors that operate to sustain racial inequality. Given the attention in the popular media and discourse that has been paid to the claim that individuals and institutions have become color-blind, the significance of this question becomes clear.

Decades of valuable survey data tell a complicated story about racial attitudes in America (see Schuman et al. 1997; Bobo et al. 2012; Krysan 2012a, b, c). Looked at from one vantage point, we *have* become "color-blind," if by "color-blind" we mean that the norms in the United States have shifted, so that it is now just a very small percentage of people who espouse explicit attitudes supporting the principles of racial inequality in housing. For example, in 1963, 60 percent of whites agreed that "white people have a right to keep blacks out of their neighborhoods if they want to, and blacks should respect that right" and by 1995, when the question was asked on a national survey for the last time, this had dropped to just 13 percent (Schuman et al. 1997).[1] Beyond this opposition to the principle of segregated neighborhoods, there has also been substantial liberalization in terms of how whites feel about living in neighborhoods with African Americans: in 1958, 45 percent of whites said they "might" or "would definitely" move if a black family moved in next door; this fell to just 2 percent of whites by the time the question was dropped from surveys (Schuman et al. 1997). The data for African Americans is sparser, but what there are show that blacks' attitudes have changed little over time, and African Americans have always been opposed to the principle of segregation, and quite open to high levels of neighborhood integration (Schuman et al. 1997).[2] But does this overwhelming opposition to the principle of segregated neighborhoods translate into a color-blind nation? A substantial body of evidence that explores this question in more nuanced and complex ways suggests that the answer is no.[3]

First, we know from other direct survey questions about housing-related issues that the virtually unanimous opposition to the principle of segregated neighborhoods is far from complete when the emphasis shifts away from principles to preferences and implementation. For example, when it comes to a nondiscrimination law that ensures whites cannot "keep blacks out" of their neighborhoods, support is not universal, nor has there been as dramatic a change over time. When white respondents were asked in 1973 to choose between the following two laws: "a law that says a homeowner can decide for himself who to sell his house to, even if he prefers not to sell to blacks" or "a

homeowner cannot refuse to sell to someone because of their race or color"
only 34 percent said they would vote for the law (the second law) that supported the principle of equality. By 2012, this had grown to a clear majority
of 70 percent. Of course, this means that it was still the case that one-third of
whites still support a law permitting discrimination against African American
homebuyers (Schuman et al. 1997; Krysan 2013).

With regard to how people feel about living in neighborhoods with people
of different races and ethnicities, the story is also more complicated and the
measurement techniques more sophisticated since the original Gallup survey
question asking if a white person would move if a black person moved next
door (Schuman et al. 1997). The Detroit Area Study has measured three times
the racial residential preferences of whites and blacks living in the Detroit
metropolitan area, and the results are revealing. Rather than asking about
a single black family moving next door, survey participants were asked to
respond to neighborhoods with a range of different racial compositions. Between 1976 and 2004, the percentage of white Detroiters who said they would
feel comfortable in a neighborhood with a 20 percent African American and
80 percent white population increased from 58 percent to 89 percent (Farley
2011). Thus, there is a growing openness among whites toward sharing a
neighborhood with African Americans. At the same time, whites are not
color-blind; they are influenced substantially by the size of the black population in the hypothetical neighborhood. For example, in 2004, whereas 88
percent of whites would be willing to move into a 7 percent black neighborhood, just 35 percent of whites would be willing to move into a 53 percent
black neighborhood.

There is little data on the attitudes of and about groups besides blacks and
whites. But Camille Charles's (2006) study of Los Angeles is an exception. In
her study, she asked whites, blacks, Latinos, and Asians to create their ideal
neighborhood racial composition. She found that whites, blacks, Asians, and
Latinos all prefer their own group to be the largest group in the neighborhood, but only for whites is their own group (whites in this case) close to
the majority of the population in the neighborhood. Additionally, for whites,
Asians, and Latinos, the least desired group is black neighbors. And across all
racial/ethnic groups, whites are the most preferred potential neighbors—with
Asians and Latinos falling in between these two extremes.

The second body of evidence we have about housing-related color blindness—or its lack thereof—comes from experiments. These range from
experiments embedded in surveys to audit studies conducted in the field.
Housing audit studies demonstrate that landlords and real estate agents are
not color-blind. In the most recent nationwide audit study that tracks housing
discrimination (Turner et al. 2013), the results are both optimistic and pes-

simistic. Certain kinds of discrimination have declined over the past twenty or so years: this includes flat-out refusals to meet with a potential renter/buyer or telling the buyer/rental that no units are available. At the same time, other forms of discrimination persist. That is, although most audit testers were shown an available unit, white renters are told about, and shown, more units than Asians, blacks, and Latinos. Similar patterns hold for homebuyers, though Latino-white differences are smaller than others, pointing to a decline in the levels of discrimination against Latino homebuyers over time.

We also know that when people evaluate neighborhoods, they are often not color-blind. We showed videos of actual neighborhoods to random samples of Chicago- and Detroit-area residents (Krysan et al. 2007). Our survey participants were randomly assigned to view white, black, or racially mixed neighborhoods—neighborhoods that were identical in every way except for the race of the individuals seen walking down the street (the "residents" were actors hired to appear in the videos). Respondents were then asked to evaluate the neighborhoods they saw. Despite being identical on every other visible attribute, whites still downgraded the evaluations of the black neighborhoods compared to the mixed, and especially all-white, neighborhoods. A similar pattern has been shown in a number of other survey-based experiments (Emerson et al. 2001; Lewis et al. 2011). For African Americans, the racial composition of the neighborhood in the video also mattered, but about one-half as much as it did for whites, and its pattern was different: African American and mixed (black/white) neighborhoods were more desirable than the all-white neighborhoods (Krysan et al. 2007).

We also know from other non-experimental survey-based studies that people's perceptions of the actual communities and neighborhoods in their metropolitan area are not color-blind. For example, even after controlling for social-class characteristics of communities, Krysan and Bader (2007) demonstrate that Detroit-area residents' perceptions of the desirability of actual communities in their metropolitan area are shaped by the race of its residents. In this study, a 10 percent increase in the proportion of white residents in a community increased whites' odds of "seriously considering" living in it by 53 percent. African Americans, for their part, were unaffected by the community's proportion white or proportion black in the same analysis. Assessments of one's own neighborhood are also shaped by the neighborhood's racial composition, above and beyond the social-class characteristics, actual crime levels, and school scores, for example, as Swaroop and Krysan (2011) show for Chicago-area residents.[4] Outside of the arena of housing, Goyette et al. (2012) have also demonstrated that whites' evaluations of the quality of neighborhood schools is impacted by changes in the racial composition of its student body. In their study of the Philadelphia metropolitan area, when the size of the black population increased in a school, white residents perceived declines in the quality of the school—even controlling for school characteristics like school poverty, test scores, and violence rates.

The studies just reviewed all go to great lengths—either through the use of sophisticated experimental designs or fancy statistical models—to establish that race, "per se," makes a difference. The reason for all this effort is because original studies about, for example, attitudes toward living in neighborhoods with people of different races/ethnicities, were criticized because it may be that the objections people (mostly whites) had weren't *really* about race but instead about social class. That is, it wasn't that white people wanted to avoid neighbors who were black. It was that they wanted to avoid the kinds of neighborhoods in which they presumed blacks lived. It wasn't an objection to black schoolchildren. It was an objection to the low performing schools they attended. It wasn't an objection to a community that had a particular percentage of African Americans. It was an objection to what they imagined the community's resources would be. It wasn't that the potential tenant was black. It was that the landlord assumed the potential black tenant could not afford to live in the unit. In other words, the argument is that people are class conscious but color-blind. To be sure, social class matters. Everybody wants to live in a neighborhood with better schools, nicer amenities, lower crime, and rising property values. Nobody expects a landlord to rent to someone who can't pay the rent. But what these powerful studies demonstrate is that race matters too—above and beyond these social-class-related concerns.

On the one hand, these studies reinforce the fallacy of our national color blindness in the area of housing and neighborhoods. We have successfully experimentally and statistically disentangled race from class and demonstrated that race continues to shape outcomes. But there is a more subtle and perhaps more pernicious way in which the issues of race and class emerge in this conversation about whether or not we are now "color-blind." It is increasingly difficult, if the goal is to understand how race operates and is understood and discussed in the United States, to conceptually (and, it turns out, in the arena of housing, even statistically) separate one from the other. Several examples, from the macro to the micro, illustrate the challenge.

For example: the effect of race *can* depend on social class. In an audit study of landlords in Philadelphia, Massey and Lundy (2001) measured the effect of race, class, and gender on housing discrimination. They had male and female testers who spoke with accents that sounded (1) lower-class black; (2) middle-class black; or (3) middle-class white. Using an experimental design, the testers inquired about an advertised rental unit and records were kept about the outcome of that inquiry. Massey and Lundy (2001) found that the worst treatment was reserved for female lower-class black testers.

Although middle-class white male testers were treated better than any of the other groups (76 percent were able to access the unit), it was also true that middle-class black males and females received better treatment (63 percent of males and 57 percent of females gained access) than their lower-class black counterparts (44 percent of males and 38 percent of females gained access). Despite this and other evidence that social class makes a difference, bear in mind the earlier observation that regardless of social class, race still operates. One need only remember Obama's speech after the verdict in the Trayvon Martin case when he recalled that he had experienced many of the same indignities as a Harvard Law School graduate, that Trayvon Martin likely had in his short life; or recall the arrest of Harvard professor and public intellectual Henry Louis Gates, as he was entering his home in an affluent neighborhood of Cambridge. Social class does not insulate middle-class blacks from "race mattering" (Feagin and Sikes 1994) but there is evidence that the consequences of being black differ depending on what social class position you occupy.

But beyond the possibility that how race operates can be influenced by one's social class there is a more subtle way that race and class are conflated in both the reality and the imaginary. For example, race and class are conflated when we look at neighborhood quality. Peterson and Krivo (2010), in their study of the effects of neighborhood racial context—independent of social class—on crime rates, were forced to assemble a *nationwide* database of neighborhoods because of the inability in a single-city study to find, on the one hand, sufficient numbers of very poor white neighborhoods and, on the other hand, enough middle-class minority neighborhoods. Only by assembling data about neighborhoods across ninety-one large U.S. cities were they able to have enough neighborhoods to permit race—net of social class—comparisons. As Sampson says of the city of Chicago:

> Not a single predominantly white neighborhood had an income level as low as that in the typical black community. Conversely, only a very small proportion of Chicago's African American neighborhoods had per capita income levels as high as those for any white area [and so] . . . trying to estimate the effect of concentrated disadvantage on whites is . . . tantamount to estimating a phantom reality. (Sampson 2009, p. 265, in Peterson and Krivo 2010, p. 40)

Even with their sample of neighborhoods in ninety-one U.S. cities, Peterson and Krivo (2010) illustrate the stark social-class differences across racially distinct neighborhoods. Figure 2.1 charts the relationship between social disadvantage and racial composition and exemplifies the "divergent social worlds" that Peterson and Krivo (2010) study. For example, 0.1 percent of black neighborhoods are as advantaged as more than one-quarter of white

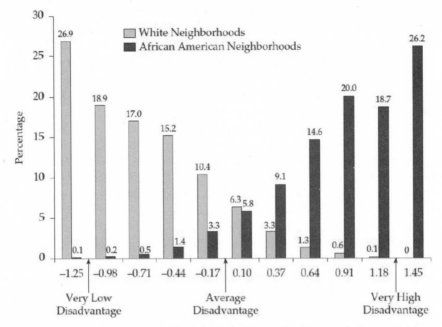

Figure 2.1. Disadvantage Distributions for White and African American Neighborhoods. Source: National Neighborhood Crime Study (Peterson and Krivo 2010).

neighborhoods. At the other extreme, there are *no* white neighborhoods that are as disadvantaged as more than one-quarter of black neighborhoods. These are "divergent social worlds" (Peterson and Krivo 2010) that cannot be reduced to race *or* class. It is virtually impossible, statistically speaking, when considering neighborhoods and communities, to talk about race in isolation or to talk about social class in isolation. Neither is reducible to the other when we are trying to understand how race operates in the United States. In the next several examples, these structural patterns of neighborhoods and the difficulty of disentangling race and class at the macro level is mirrored by challenges to do the same at the more micro level.

These kernels of truth—created by the structural racism that results in these divergent social worlds (Peterson and Krivo 2010) for blacks and whites in particular—contribute to and are reinforced by a constellation of attitudes and beliefs among individuals that are equally complicated by this race/class issue. For example, this kernel of truth about minority neighborhoods is reflected in white attitudes about racially integrated neighborhoods (Krysan et al. 2008). Not only are such places viewed as overall less desirable (Krysan et al. 2007), but they are also imbued with a set of characteristics and stereotypes about what their qualities are. We see this when we consider the video experiment reported earlier. In addition to asking about the overall desirability of the neighborhoods portrayed in the videos, survey participants were also asked to rate the neighborhoods on a number of different dimensions based solely on the visual representation of the neighborhood: the upkeep of the property, quality of schools, level of crime, cost of housing, and likelihood that property values would increase (Krysan et al. 2008). Whites evaluated neighborhoods with black residents as less safe, having worse schools, lower housing values, and being less likely to increase in property values. African Americans were also influenced by neighborhood racial composition, though the effects were more complex and depended on the characteristic being rated. For example, neighborhood racial composition did not influence African Americans' perceptions of home values or safety of the neighborhood but white and mixed neighborhoods were perceived as having better schools than all-black neighborhoods. And it was mixed neighborhoods that were viewed as having the best prospects for future housing values (Krysan et al. 2008). In short, the neighborhood racial composition conjured up in residents' minds— especially whites—a number of social-class-related characteristics.

The same set of inferences was apparent in another study (Krysan 2002) that allowed white survey participants to describe in their own words the reasons why they would be likely to move out of a racially integrated neighborhood (assuming they said they would). When asked why they would leave a neighborhood that came to have more African American residents than they were comfortable with, a substantial number of white residents in Atlanta, Boston, Detroit, and Los Angeles indicated that they would leave because of a variety of explicitly racial reasons. For example: "Because I'd be uncomfortable. [What do you mean?] What can I say, I just don't like blacks." And: "I'd feel I was being moved out of my neighborhood"; and "They are lazy and dirty" (Krysan 2002). But the most common set of concerns raised by respondents who were explaining why they would leave an integrated neighborhood intertwined race and class and are what were referred to as "race-associated" reasons. Take these three examples:

"The houses will go downhill. When one moves in, a lot of things come along with it."
"The market value of our property would drop quick."
"I wouldn't want to live in a rundown neighborhood with drugs, violence, crime and that's how the neighborhood would change."

These stereotypes held by whites about the neighborhoods in which African Americans live illustrate the close connection in whites' minds between race and class when it comes to residence. Just because respondents invoke social-class reasons for their racial preferences, this does not mean that they are nonracial. Nor does it mean that they are unrelated to social class. As noted above, neither is reducible to the other. In her study of working-class men in the United States and France, Lamont (2000) highlights how the very definition of racial boundaries has come to be infused with social-class characteristics.

In a recent essay, Elijah Anderson (2012) provides a powerful discussion of how this conflation of race and class in the minds of Americans is deeply consequential. In doing so, though not his direct purpose, he demonstrates another way in which neighborhoods and housing are implicated in any discussion of racial inequality. His focus is on how race relations in general—and the experiences of African Americans in particular—are shaped so profoundly by what he calls the iconic ghetto. As he writes (2012, p. 8):

> In the minds of many Americans, the ghetto is "where the black people live," symbolizing an impoverished, crime-prone, drug-infested, and violent area of the city. Aided by the mass media and popular culture, this image of the ghetto has achieved an iconic status, and serves as a powerful source of stereotype, prejudice, and discrimination.

The inextricable linking of "where black people live" with the "ghetto" (and all of the negative social characteristics associated with the ghetto) is consequential in that it is someplace to be avoided. This is consistent with the studies reported above where whites in particular hold a very race/class imbued understanding of communities and neighborhoods that have more than a few African American residents (for example, Krysan et al. 2008; Krysan 2002). But the consequences of the "iconic ghetto" extend far beyond where people live or want to live, to how black people, regardless of their actual class position, are treated in interracial interactions. White people in particular, Anderson (2012) argues, understand African Americans they meet (especially in racially mixed or predominantly white areas) as people who embody the ghetto. As Anderson (2012, p. 17) puts it: "When whites encounter a black stranger in public, the iconic ghetto almost invariably serves as a reference point to interpret his or her identity and the import of his or her presence." Thus, individual African Americans cannot escape the presumption that they are "of the ghetto" and this creates a situation where black people are forever trying to shed the associations with the ghetto. Anderson (2012, p. 17) notes: "the association of black skin with the powerful image of the ghetto can easily overwhelm the black person's best efforts and attract closer scrutiny, as whites struggle to recalibrate their interactions with the anonymous black person." Individual African Americans cannot escape the iconic ghetto in their daily lives—regardless of whether they are physically "of" or "in" the ghetto. And whites don't want to come near the iconic ghetto. As such, neighborhood race and class are inextricably linked in the housing decisions people make, and, Anderson (2012) notes, this imagery also powerfully shapes the nature and quality of relations between blacks and whites. These interactions that are shaped by the iconic ghetto serve to undermine efforts to create racial equality and integrated communities.

It is hard to understand the body of evidence presented here as anything but racial. There is no post-racial. There is no color-blind. Race is conflated with class in complicated ways, but it has not become conveniently all about social class. It is about race *and* class. To reclaim and undo this conflation requires that we disentangle them in reality and in perception—not just in a social experiment or audit study. Stereotypes need undoing. People need to forge relationships across racial/ethnic boundaries. Investments need to be made in neighborhoods and communities so that the kernel of truth is eliminated. It is not adequate to simply "fix up" the people, neighborhoods, and communities. We know that the racial background of a home seeker matters, outside of her or his ability to afford a home (Turner et al. 2013). We know that racial composition of a school matters, outside of the quality of its programs (Goyette et al. 2012). We know racial composition of the neighborhood matters, outside of its social-class characteristics (Emerson et al. 2001; Krysan et al. 2007). In short, we know that people are not color-blind; and we need to take that into account when we think about how to solve the myriad social problems created by segregated housing—and, by extension, segregated schools.

NOTES

1. Although trend data are unavailable (the same question was not asked in repeated surveys over time), it is instructive to also note that in 1942, fully 85 percent of whites supported the principle of segregated housing (Krysan 2012a).

2. For example, between 1980 and 1996, the percentage of African Americans who agreed that "white people have a right to keep blacks out of their neighborhoods if they want to, and blacks should respect that right" went from 16 percent to 3 percent (Schuman et al. 1997).

3. This review, by focusing on housing in particular, necessarily sidesteps the growing body of research that has identified "implicit" or "unconscious" racial attitudes. These are attitudes that operate outside of individual consciousness and that shape (in a negative fashion) intergroup relations. This body of research makes a compelling case for the existence of these subtle biases, and it is likely that they play a role in some of the results we report on how race shapes perceptions of neighborhoods. Nevertheless, because implicit attitudes research has not targeted housing-related attitudes, and due to space constraints, I do not include a detailed discussion of

this topic except to acknowledge it as an important line of research and social process. For a review see Fazio and Olson (2003).

4. The Swaroop and Krysan (2011) results contradict some earlier studies of the relationship between racial composition and neighborhood satisfaction, controlling for social-class characteristics (Harris 1999; 2001; Taub et al. 1984). A key difference is that Swaroop and Krysan (2011) relied on objective measures of social class (census data, data on crime reports, and school test scores) whereas earlier studies that showed no effect of racial composition used respondents' reports of social-class-related characteristics.

REFERENCES

Anderson, Elijah. 2012. "The Iconic Ghetto." *Annals of the American Academy of Political and Social Science* 642: 8–24.

Bobo, Lawrence D. 1989. "Keeping the Linchpin in Place: Testing the Multiple Sources of Opposition to Residential Integration." *International Review of Social Psychology* 2: 305–23.

Bobo, Lawrence D., Camille Z. Charles, Maria Krysan, and Alicia D. Simmons. 2012. "The *Real* Record on Racial Attitudes." In *Social Trends in American Life: Findings from the General Social Survey since 1972*, edited by Peter V. Marsden (pp. 38–83). Princeton, NJ: Princeton University Press.

Charles, Camille Z. 2006. *Won't You Be My Neighbor? Race, Class, and Residence in Los Ángeles*. New York: Russell Sage Foundation.

Emerson, Michael O., George Yancey, and Karen J. Chai. 2001. "Does Race Matter in Residential Segregation? Exploring the Preferences of White Americans." *American Sociological Review* 66(6): 922–35.

Farley, Reynolds. 2011. "The Waning of American Apartheid." *Contexts: Understanding People in their Social Worlds* 10(3): 36–43.

Fazio, Russell H., and Michael A. Olson. 2003. "Implicit Measures in Social Cognition Research: Their Meaning and Use." *Annual Review of Psychology* 54: 297–327.

Feagin, Joe R., and Melvin P. Sikes. 1994. *Living with Racism: The Black Middle-Class Experience*. Boston, MA: Beacon Press.

Goyette, Kimberly A., Danielle Farrie, and Joshua Freely. 2012. "This School's Gone Downhill: Racial Change and Perceived School Quality among Whites." *Social Problems* 59(2): 155–76.

Harris, David. R. 1999. "'Property Values Drop When Blacks Move In, Because. . .': Racial and Socioeconomic Determinants of Neighborhood Desirability." *American Sociological Review* 64: 461–79.

Harris, David. R. 2001. "Why Are Whites and Blacks Averse to Black Neighbors?" *Social Science Research* 30: 100–116.

Krysan, Maria, and Michael Bader. 2007. "Perceiving the Metropolis: Seeing the City through a Prism of Race." *Social Forces* 86(2): 699–733.

Krysan, Maria, Reynolds Farley, and Mick P. Couper. 2008. "In the Eye of the Beholder: Racial Beliefs and Residential Segregation." *DuBois Review* 5(1): 5–26.

Krysan, Maria, Reynolds Farley, Mick P. Couper, and Tyrone Forman. 2007. "Does Race Matter in Neighborhood Preferences? Results from a Video Experiment." *American Journal of Sociology* 115(2): 527–669.

Krysan, Maria. 2002. "Whites Who Say They'd Flee: Who Are They and Why Would They Leave?" *Demography* 39(4): 675–96.

Krysan, Maria. 2012a. "From Color Caste to Color Blind, Part I: Racial Attitudes in the United States during World War II, 1978–1945." In *The Oxford Handbook of African American Citizenship, 1865–Present*, edited by Henry Louis Gates Jr., Claude Steele, Lawrence D. Bobo, Gerald Jaynes, Lisa Crooms-Robinson, and Linda Darling-Hammond (pp. 195–234). New York: Oxford University Press.

Krysan, Maria. 2012b. "From Color Caste to Color Blind, Part II: Racial Attitudes in the United States During the Civil Rights and Black Power Eras, 1946–1975." In T*he Oxford Handbook of African American Citizenship, 1865–Present*, edited by Henry Louis Gates Jr., Claude Steele, Lawrence D. Bobo, Gerald Jaynes, Lisa Crooms-Robinson, and Linda Darling-Hammond (pp. 195–234). New York: Oxford University Press.

Krysan, Maria. 2012c. "From Color Caste to Color Blind, Part III: Contemporary Era Racial Attitudes, 1976–2004." In *The Oxford Handbook of African American Citizenship, 1865–Present*, edited by Henry Louis Gates Jr., Claude Steele, Lawrence D. Bobo, Gerald Jaynes, Lisa Crooms-Robinson, and Linda Darling-Hammond (pp. 235–75). New York: Oxford University Press.

Lamont, Michele. 2000. *The Dignity of Working Men: Morality and the Boundaries of Race, Class, and Immigration*. New York: Russell Sage Foundation.

Lewis, Valerie A., Michael O. Emerson, and Stephen L. Klineberg. 2011. "Who We'll Live With: Neighborhood Racial Composition Preferences of Whites, Blacks, and Latinos." *Social Forces* 89(4): 1385–1407.

Massey, Douglas S., and Garvey Lundy. 2001. "Use of Black English and Racial Discrimination in Urban Housing Markets." *Urban Affairs Review* 36(4): 452–69.

Peterson, Ruth D., and Lauren J. Krivo. 2010. *Divergent Social Worlds: Neighborhood Crime and the Racial-Spatial Divide*. New York: Russell Sage Foundation.

Pettigrew, Thomas F. 1979. "Racial Change and Social Policy." *Annals of the American Academy of Political and Social Science* 441: 114–31.

Sampson, Robert J. 2009. "Racial Stratification and the Durable Tangle of Neighborhood Inequality." *Annals of the American Academy of Political and Social Science* 621(1): 260–80.

Schuman, Howard, Charlotte Steeh, Lawrence Bobo, and Maria Krysan. 1997. *Racial Attitudes in America: Trends and Interpretations, Revised Edition.* Cambridge, MA: Harvard University Press.

Swaroop, Sapna, and Maria Krysan. 2011. "The Determinants of Neighborhood Satisfaction: Racial Prejudice and Racial Proxy Revisited." *Demography* 48: 1203–29.

Taub, Robert P., D. Garth Taylor, and Jan D. Dunham. 1984. *Paths of Neighborhood Change: Race and Crime in Urban America.* Chicago: University of Chicago Press.

Turner, Margery Austin, Rob Santos, Diane K. Levy, Doug Wissoker, Claudia
   Aranda, and Rob Pitingolo. 2013. *Housing Discrimination against Racial and
   Ethnic Minorities 2012: Executive Summary*. Washington, DC: U.S. Department
   of Housing and Urban Development, Office of Policy Development and Research.

Chapter Three

A Different Story

Race, Politics, and Radical Change

Eddie Glaude Jr.

Perhaps if we learn more of what has happened and why it happened, we'll learn more of who we really are. And perhaps if we learn more about our unwritten history, we won't be so vulnerable to the capriciousness of events as we are today.

—Ralph Ellison

The 1980s and 1990s laid the foundation for the way race works in the United States today. Ronald Reagan solidified a national approach to race that effectively shifted the burden of redress from the state to black people themselves. These shifts still frame American politics—especially so, with its first black president. The 1980s and 1990s were the decades where color blindness became a dominant theme in the mouths of conservatives and a prominent feature in the mind-numbing triangulation of Bill Clinton–inspired liberals, where the issues that once exercised American political debate (affirmative action, crime, welfare, etc.) began to fall off the radar screen as an unspoken national consensus was reached among white fellow citizens about how best to address race; where racial inequality, for some, resulted from individual irresponsibility and a culture of poverty; and, finally, where easy appeals to black solidarity collapsed in the face of deepening class divisions within African American communities.

Behind these events resides the long history of our national struggle with race. Any invocation of color blindness, for example, recalls, implicitly at least, Justice Harlan's dissent to *Plessy v. Ferguson*, the 1896 Supreme Court decision that established separate but equal as the law of the land. Justice Harlan wrote, "In respect of civil rights to all citizens, the constitution of the United States does not, I think, permit any public authority to know the race of those entitled to be protected in the enjoyment of such rights." Any appeal to a culture of poverty—that troublesome description of personal choices and habits that, according to some, frustrate genuine opportunity for black communities—contains the residual trace of Daniel Patrick Moynihan's 1965 declaration that "the fundamental problem [with the Negro] is that of the family structure." Of course, these moments are haunted by the ghosts of slavery, by the reasons given for generations to hold other human beings in bondage, and by the necessity to "close ranks" in the face of their often horrible consequences.

In no way am I suggesting that race holds constant over the course of U.S. history. Race is made in the context of human doings and sufferings; it has its beginnings as a metaphor that enables us to render the complexity of the world's inhabitants in such a way that seems manageable—at least for the moment. Race, in other words, is not some fixed or static thing that crops up whole over the course of our living. It is a tool of language, and it happens to be one that carries with it "stuff" from previous struggles, buildup that gathers around the word like food particles around teeth. How we account for and tend to that "stuff" is critically important—especially today.

What I aim to do in this brief essay is twofold. I show that a particularly narrow story of racial progress blocks the way to a more substantive engagement with racial inequality in this country. That story begins with the abolition of slavery, embraces a certain version of the civil rights movement, and culminates in the election of Barack Obama. It is a story that affirms the inherent goodness of the nation by hiding from view (through a delicate balance of remembering and forgetting) the nastier dimensions of our racial history. I specifically point to the ways Ronald Reagan's support of a national holiday for Dr. Martin Luther King Jr. effectively contained and, in some cases, undermined the broader quest for racial justice. More specifically, Dr. King's "I Have a Dream" speech becomes a rhetorical resource for the ideal of color blindness that conceals how race continues to disadvantage certain groups in this country. I then examine what follows from this distinctive use of Dr. King and the invocation of color blindness. In the end, I suggest that something much more fundamental has to happen if we are to genuinely pursue racial justice in this country: we have to reimagine who we are as a nation. As such, the idea of integration only offers a substantive remedy to racial inequality if the very notion of American democracy is unhinged from an idea of "whiteness" that distorts it.

Our historical memory bears the traces (or "stuff") of our national neurosis around race. The neurosis stems from the undeniable fact that our claims to democracy have always been shadowed by our commitments, implicit and otherwise, to "whiteness": the belief that white Americans matter more because they are white, and that this value should be evident in the political economy of the nation. I am not suggesting that we are a nation of "explicit racists." Poll data consistently show that most white Americans, when asked, hold commitments consistent with the value of racial equality. But we have been habituated to live race in a particular way, and those habits, let's call them *racial habits*, reproduce inequalities and indifference that frustrate the life chances of a large number of Americans. Even as white Americans acknowledge the wrongness of racial inequality, most oppose government policies designed to remedy that inequality. So, while the norms of white supremacy have been discarded for explicit commitments to the norms of antidiscrimination, we still confront the undeniable fact that America is as segregated as ever and that fact disproportionately affects the life chances of large numbers of Americans.

For example, we know, according to Census 2000 data, that half of African Americans live in "hypersegregated" census tracts and that segregation disadvantages those who live in such places. It impacts their access "to public and private resources . . . , depresses their ability to accumulate wealth and gain access to credit,"[1] and narrows the range of networks that offer pathways to social and cultural capital. In short, we know that segregation drives a number of differential outcomes that disadvantage particular groups. But, because of the story we have told ourselves about our struggles with race and racism in this country—a story that hinges on the idea of racial progress that affirms our inherent goodness as a nation—we refuse to look the ugliness of contemporary forms of segregation squarely in the face by hiding behind the ideal of color blindness. What is all too clear, at least to me, is that racial inequality functions today under the sign of the post-racial or through appeals to color blindness. That is, the denial of the significance of race today perpetuates the disadvantage particular groups face *because* of race. The irony, of course, is that this happens in the context of the historical election of our first African American president.

Most Americans reveled in the historical significance of the 2008 presidential election. Barack Obama's election supposedly signaled the end of *white democracy* (the idea that the benefits and burdens of citizenship accrue to persons differentially according to their skin; that whiteness as a political and moral category carries with it a range of opportunities and privileges that reflect the unique position of white people in our politics, giving added weight to their concerns and voice in our national conversation).[2] His election, with all of its implications for the future, necessitated a return to the past—a need to tell a story about how such an event was possible. Novelty requires nothing less. It demands an account of itself, and memory and history are its central tools. But Americans have a tendency, especially when it comes to black folk, to turn a blind eye to the past. Such forgetting protects our national innocence and buries our complicity in collective injustice. Ralph Ellison described this as part of a "national fantasy of an America free of blacks." And, for Ellison, this deep desire was "born not merely of racism but petulance, exasperation and moral fatigue."[3]

With Obama's election we told ourselves a story of racial progress. From the abolition of slavery to Rosa Parks's refusal to give up her seat to Dr. King's "I Have a Dream" speech at the 1963 March on Washington to the election of Obama himself, the American drama of race was one of progressive alignment with the country's precious ideals of democracy. Of course, that story ignored much of the ugliness of the past and glossed over its implication in our present. It limited the complicated nature of black political activism (black power was anathema or Rosa Parks's activism, before and after her refusal to give up her seat, was erased) and ignored the ongoing white resistance to the demands of that struggle. To be sure, Obama's election fed into what the historian David Blight calls "a mythos of accomplished glory, a history of emancipation completed." Obama's victory not only trumped race matters in our current moment, his election, for some, bludgeoned the problem of race out of American history altogether.[4] It was as if, on the steps of the Capitol, with each repeated word of the Oath of Office, scenes of our racial past faded from view. Here the archive—the past itself—became as color-blind (or whitewashed) as we now claim to be, and the blues voices of old and their democratic yearnings were barely audible.

Our use of the past can work differently. "[V]isions of the good life can come from recollections and reconstructions of the past, not only from fantasies of the future."[5] Utopian imaginings aren't our only recourse. Visions can emerge from our attempts to forge a new America, not one beholden to a narrow exceptionalism that justifies our ugliness, but from an understanding of ourselves that grows out of a serious and sustained confrontation with how ugly we have been and can be. Just as exploring the depths of long, buried memories can release a troubled person into a higher form of self, a genuine encounter with the past can enable a transformation in the idea of who we take ourselves to be as a nation. This is a different kind of remedy of the effects of segregation. It is not a call for integration; rather, it is a demand for a fundamental reimagining of America itself, and that reimagining begins with a different story about America's recent past.

On November 2, 1983, President Ronald Reagan, on a nice autumn day in the White House Rose Garden, signed the bill instituting the Martin Luther King Jr. holiday into law. Reagan invoked the words of John Greenleaf Whittier, one of the Fireside Poets, a Quaker and an ardent abolitionist. He quoted a line from Whittier's 1880 poem, *The Lost Occasion*: "Each crisis brings its words and deed." Reagan told a brief story of the civil rights movement, a story that confirmed for him the "sense that true justice must be color-blind, and that among white and black Americans, as [King] put it, [t]heir destiny is tied up with our destiny, and their freedom is inextricably bound to our freedom; we cannot walk alone." It was a familiar story—one that began with Rosa Parks's defiant act in Montgomery, Alabama, included the March on Washington, and ended in the passage of the Voting Rights Act of 1964 and the Civil Rights Act of 1965.

King's holiday became an occasion to affirm a certain vision of the country, to insist on the power of our democratic values, and to express faith in our promised future. Reagan said:

> Now our nation has decided to honor Dr. Martin Luther King, Jr. by setting aside a day each year to remember him and the just cause he stood for. We've made historic strides since Rosa Parks refused to go to the back of the bus. As a democratic people, we can take pride in the knowledge that we Americans recognized a grave injustice and took action to correct it. And we should remember that in far too many countries, people like Dr. King never have the opportunity to speak out at all.

Reagan brilliantly drafted King's sacrifice and all of those who participated in the civil rights movement into a broader story of American exceptionalism: that sense of our nation, no matter its shortcomings, as a singular place where liberty, equality, and individuality flourish under the watchful eyes of God. These were the tropes of America's civil religion, where patriotism expressed itself as a commitment to the divine favor bestowed upon our nation and its sacred role in geopolitical matters. As Reagan concluded his remarks, he quoted Samuel Francis Smith's "My Country 'Tis of Thee," words King invoked in the "I Have a Dream" speech: "All of God's children will be able to sing with new meaning," Reagan said, "land where my fathers died, land of the pilgrim's pride, from every mountainside, let freedom ring." With these words, Reagan ushered King into our national pantheon. He was now, although many remained suspicious, a true patriot.

The scene in the Rose Garden carried with it a biting sense of irony. For many African Americans, Reagan's election represented a national retreat on civil rights; he was the poster child of a disturbing white backlash. Reagan's attack on affirmative action, his calls for constructive engagement with the apartheid regime of South Africa, his evisceration of the Equal Employment Opportunity Commission (EEOC) and the U.S. Commission on Civil Rights, all in the name of color blindness, made him the most unlikely supporter of a national holiday for Dr. King. What stood out for Reagan and other conservatives was not King's rejection of "interposition and nullification (key weapons in the states' rights arsenal); it was his dream of a day when all

Americans would be *judged not by the color of their skin but by the content of their character*. Individuals mattered, not groups or their particular histories.

Ironically King's words aided the national process of turning a blind eye to the legacies of white supremacy and the persistence of racial inequality. For some, the holiday effectively washed our national hands clean; the sins of our racial past gave way to an emphasis on individual merit and responsibility. And persistent racial inequality was seen, not as the result of racist policies or actual discrimination but, rather, racial inequality was the result of a culture of poverty, which produced bad or, minimally, irresponsible people. Moreover, any reference to race in public policy debates, to acknowledge the significance of racial and cultural differences in the public domain or the effects of historic racism in areas like employment or education, was subject to claims of reverse racism or accusations of trading in victimology talk. In short, the King holiday inaugurated a *new racial contract*.

The philosopher Charles Mills put forward the idea that "the racial contract" ought to be understood as a signature feature of Western societies: that whites enter into a set of formal and informal agreements with each other in order to secure for themselves the privileges and advantages of the social contract while maintaining the subordination and exploitation of nonwhites. As Mills argues: "the general purpose of the Contract is always the differential privileging of the whites as a group with respect to the nonwhites as a group, the exploitation of their bodies, land, and resources, and the denial of equal socioeconomical opportunities to them. All whites are beneficiaries of the Contract, though some whites are not signatories to it."[6] To be sure, delineating the features of the racial contract helps isolate the complex ways in which whiteness impacts the distribution of benefits and burdens in supposedly democratic societies. It makes sense that in the Jim Crow South certain assumptions about whiteness and its benefits inform the shaping of policy. The same thing is evidenced in northern cities with, for example, racially restrictive covenants in which a legal obligation was imposed by the seller upon the buyer of real estate that they could not sell the property to African Americans. Mills tends to think about the racial contract only in this way: as a set of formal and informal agreements that benefit whites and harm nonwhites.

The new racial contract has to be thought of differently. Jim Crow signs are no more. Racially restrictive covenants are illegal. And, for the most part, there is a general public consensus that overt racism—a kind of explicit defense of white supremacy—is no longer tolerable. In other words, there has been a publicly voiced commitment to the value of racial equality, and color blindness is its central trope. However, the new racial contract demands a concession on the part of black folk. Not that they must concede the superiority of whiteness and the inferiority of blackness explicitly, but that the condition for acceptance into mainstream American society is the renunciation of a previous idea of black identity that calls into question whiteness, a kind of forgetting of past experiences that may color present living if one is to be accepted fully into American society. Here the idea of whiteness is maintained not by coercion but by *our* consent: where the alluring appeal of mainstream acceptance results in our inability to give voice freely to *our* difference and its implication for living in twenty-first-century America. And, to my mind, Dr. King's holiday and his "I Have a Dream" speech have become the key symbols for this new contract.

The social imaginary that once lent a semblance of coherence to lives shadowed by the specter of racism has now collapsed. This collapse has occurred, ironically, under the weight of the success of a particular quest for black freedom and its story. That is to say, the civic mythology of the civil rights movement—a story that equates Martin Luther King Jr.'s "dream" and, by extension, black people's political desire with the aims of America itself—contains within it a death warrant for black America. There is the idea, and it has been a cruel feature of a certain liberal vision of American politics, that the price for wholesale inclusion in American life for black people is that they, once and for all, leave behind any attachments to who they are *as black people*. James Baldwin clearly understood the cost of this demand. With the voice of a white narrator, he wrote in "Many Thousands Gone,"

> Time has made some changes in the Negro face. Nothing has succeeded in making it exactly like our own, though the general desire seems to be to make it blank if one cannot make it white. When it has become blank, the past as thoroughly washed from the black face as it has been from ours, our guilt will be finished—at least it will have ceased to be visible, which we imagine to be much the same thing.[7]

Baldwin understood this erasure as a form of dehumanization that doubled back onto white fellow citizens. As he put the point, "the loss of our own identity is the price we pay for our annulment of his." This insight illuminates our current moment in a unique way: blackness no longer signifies, among other matters, the contradiction of American ideals but, if it is to register any public meaning at all, affirms the normative values of America as such.

On its face, such a goal seems laudable. But, its more insidious effects rest in the presupposition that black people cannot be black people *and* Americans—at least, in any politically viable sense. President Obama, for example, cannot be seen as a black president in any sense other than as an affirmation of our progress toward a more perfected union. His face projects the notion, globally and domestically, that the ugliness of our racial past no longer holds. Here blackness cannot register anything other than American exceptionalism (or, perhaps, a commodity for consumption). Politically, it must be King's dream or else it is rejected as a puerile form of identity politics, a politics of victimization, or simply reverse racism.

Under present conditions what can be seen as the idols of a black freedom narrative often obscure the complex realities that shape racial inequality in the twenty-first century. We have to reject the insidious work of color-blind talk. Instead, we must name explicitly the various ways people of color suffer in this country, and we must resist efforts to avoid the discomfort that such naming all too often generates. The rhetoric of lifting all boats is not the answer. Such an approach leaves in place the devastating segregation that literally cordons off public and private resources from groups of Americans, abandoning them in opportunity deserts. Such an approach to racial inequality also leaves at the heart of our national self-conception an idea of whiteness that is the source of the disease of the American soul.

In 1944, Ralph Ellison wrote a review of Gunner Myrdal's *An American Dilemma* for *Antioch Review*. Ellison claimed that Myrdal's book had achieved some good but, in the end, reproduced the tragic flaw at the heart of our national self-conception. On the one hand, he agreed with Myrdal that we needed to expand the very idea of America to include more fully African Americans. But, on the other hand, Ellison suggested something much more radical: that if the idea of America entailed, since its inception, the belief in the inferiority of black folk and practices of their exclusion, then talk of black self-determination and full inclusion necessarily involved a fundamentally different idea of American democracy itself. The point here is not simply including black folks into American society as it is—a basic idea of integration; *it is really about rethinking the very mechanics of democracy*. Ellison wrote, and the formulation is an extraordinary one even today, that

> the solution of the problem of the American Negro and democracy lies only partially in the white man's free will. Its full solution will lie *in the creation of a democracy* in which the Negro will be free to define himself for what he is and, within the large framework of democracy, for what he desires to be.[8] (emphasis added)

To take up Myrdal's approach is to protect a certain idea of American life that is most in need of correction. Integration does not uproot the basic habits of whiteness that distort American life. Rosa Parks put the point bluntly, "I have never been what you would call just an integrationist. I know I've been called that. . . . Integrating that bus wouldn't mean more equality. Even when there was segregation there was plenty of integration in the south, but it was for the benefit and convenience of the white person, not us. So it is not just integration." The goal was "to discontinue all forms of oppression against all those who are weak and oppressed."[9] What is needed is "a change of the basis of society." If we fail in this task (the task of fundamentally reimagining America), Ellison argued, a study like Myrdal's could be "used for less democratic purposes." We now know this to be true, and what is most startling is that even the aspirational claims of Dr. King have been used for less democratic purposes. In so many ways, he and the movement out of which he comes have "become an instrument of an American tragedy"[10] that keeps us sleepwalking. Telling a different story is the beginning of waking up.

NOTES

1. Elizabeth Anderson, *The Imperative of Integration* (Princeton, NJ: Princeton University Press, 2013), 2.

2. Jason Morgan Ward, *Defending White Democracy: The Making of a Segregationist Movement and the Remaking of Racial Politics, 1936–1965* (Chapel Hill: University of North Carolina Press, 2011).

3. Ralph Ellison, "What Would American Be Like without Blacks," in *The Collected Essays of Ralph Ellison*, ed. John F. Callahan (New York: Modern Library, 2003), 581.

4. David Blight, *Race and Reunion: The Civil War in American Memory* (Cambridge, MA: Belknap Press of Harvard University Press, 2002), 237.

5. T. J. Jackson Lears, "Looking Backward," *Lingua Franca*, December–January, 1998, 66.

6. Charles Mills, *The Racial Contract* (Ithaca, NY: Cornell University Press, 1999), 11.

7. James Baldwin, *Notes of a Native Son* (Boston: Beacon Press, 1955), 25–26.

8. Ralph Ellison, *"An American Dilemma*: A Review," in *The Collected Essays of Ralph Ellison*, ed. John F. Callahan (New York: Modern Library, 2003), 328–29.

9. Quoted in Jeanne Theoharis, *The Rebellions Life of Mrs. Rosa Parks* (Boston: Beacon Press, 2013), 70.

10. Ellison, *"An American Dilemma,"* 340.

Chapter Four

The 1 Percent Needs Race to Rule

Howard Winant

Yes Virginia, there is a racial regime, a system of rule based on race. This is not really news. It is so obvious, so taken for granted, that we react with a shrug when it is pointed out. Sure, there is a racial regime. Of course. So what?

A few decades ago, when the civil rights movement was at its height, this would have been quite obvious. Going back in historical time, we find that the racial regime was openly discussed, and that those who ruled—*los que mandan*—worked assiduously to strengthen it. In the slavery era, the Jim Crow era, there was no real question about this. But what about now, in the "post-civil rights" era? Now we're color-blind, right?

Although the racial regime has been in place since the "discovery" of the Americas, since the onset of African slavery, it has never been stable. It has always been subject to challenge; it has been forced over and over to reform itself, yet it has never been destroyed. With each reform, each time it was challenged at the cost of enormous amounts of blood, sweat, and tears, the racial regime emerged fortified. Even the Civil War and Reconstruction, a quasi-revolutionary bloodletting that extended citizenship rights to formerly chattelized blacks, failed to undo the pervasive racism of American society. If that monumental upheaval, which took seven hundred fifty thousand lives (when the country's population was only about forty million), could not overcome the racial regime, why should we expect that the post–World War II racial upheavals, the marches and sit-ins and rebellions that shaped our political lives and reshaped U.S. society in so many important ways, would end it?

Yet reform matters. Although the U.S. racial regime endures, it has been sharply reconfigured. In our own time, no less than in the era of the abolition of slavery, racial transformation has been extraordinary. Hegemony, the Italian Marxist Antonio Gramsci said, involves the incorporation of opposition by the ruling class.

Here's what we have to remember: The powers that be, the ruling class, *los que mandan*, whatever you want to call them, need race to rule. Despite all the pious invocations of "color blindness," despite the Supreme Court's long-term project of redefining discrimination as something that happens mainly to white people, despite President Obama's insistence that he is not the "black president" but the president of the United States who happens to be black, and despite a hundred other examples I could give you, racial difference and racial inequality—or more properly, racism and white supremacy—remain key dimensions of the U.S. power structure.

"They"—the powerful, the 1 percent—need race to accumulate wealth. They need race to rule. The great recession that commenced in 2008, and that we are still in, could not have happened without a series of racist practices and social structures rooted in racial segregation and super-exploitation of black people particularly, but also brown people, red people, and yellow people—to use the always absurd color categories.

They need race to make war. War is itself an important source of wealth. The U.S. wars in Iraq and Afghanistan could not have happened if we still had a conscription-based army, as Charles Rangel among others pointed out. You need "volunteer" armed forces for aggressive (aka "preemptive") war: armed forces made up in large measure of low-income people who are looking for education and a career. Presidents simply cannot be so aggressive if they have a conscripted army (marines, navy, air force). The draft, though problematic in many ways, is a lot more democratic than an "all-volunteer" army is. Incidentally, the armed forces remain the major affirmative action institution in the country, the only major institution where mandatory desegregation has taken place.

In addition the assault on many of our major cities like Detroit (and Philly, where I worked and lived for twenty years), could not have happened without race and racism. No surprise there; urban segregation and white flight to the suburbs was largely engineered after World War II. It was white flight to the suburbs that shaped the two Gulf Wars, the invasion of Afghanistan, the 1953 U.S.-organized antidemocratic coup in Iran, and many other similar actions. Why is that? Because the cheap gas needed to fuel (literally) the commute from the suburbs had to be extracted by imperial interventions in the Persian Gulf and elsewhere.

For many of the same reasons, the climate crisis and global warming would not have happened without race and racism. White flight, suburban growth, and urban decay, then, were all premised on cheap oil made available by the exercise of racial repression at home and the use of U.S. military power in the colonies and post-colonies abroad. The various manifestations of the "energy crisis," including today's fracking, tar sands, acidification of the oceans (soon there may be no more fish) all owe their origins to white flight, at least in part.

The education and health care crises we currently face could not have happened without the continuing use of race for the purposes of rule. Social investment and state provision of jobs, infrastructural investment, and collective consumption goods (things like public transportation, public education, national health insurance) cannot be fully extended to the cities (that is, to black and brown people) without risks for whites, especially those in charge. Quality education is particularly dangerous to those in power. Decarceration on a serious scale would also be dangerous for the regime, both economically (where are the jobs for ex-felons?) and politically. As Michelle Alexander has pointed out, more black men are incarcerated now than were enslaved at the beginning of the Civil War (Alexander 2012).

The repression that we are experiencing as police profiling, as stop and frisk and "show me your papers" policies, and above all as mass incarceration, could not have happened without the need to rule by means of race. The contemporary political right in the United States came into being after the black movement and its allies threatened to create real democracy and redistribute income and wealth. This is how neoliberalism was invented—in California in the 1970s—with the attack on the public sector, the tax revolt, and the politics of racial fear and law and order. The white oligarchs who rule this country—the .01 percent—could very possibly have been swept aside after 1968, if they had not made a determined commitment to sustain the racial domination and racial inequality upon which this country (and to a great extent the modern world-system) was founded. The assassinations, the combination of repression and small-scale racial reform unleashed under Nixon, and most centrally the "post–civil rights era" rearticulation of the meaning of race (see below) created the racial contradictions with which we still struggle today.

I could continue with this list indefinitely, but I'll end with just one more example of the centrality of race in the U.S. political regime: electoral politics. Conflict over the franchise remains a central issue in U.S. politics, as it has since the founding of the republic. The two major political parties are racial parties: though both are corporate, the Republicans are the white party, the Democrats the multiracial party. The country's electoral geography is highly racialized: urban/rural, North/South, intermountain west/Aztlán (that's where I live and work now: Aztlán). Numerous electoral strategies are shaped by race: notably gerrymandering and "vote-caging." Race informs current Republican efforts to restrict voting for low-income people, students, inmates and ex-felons, and immigrants. Manza and Uggen (2006) estimate that without ex-felon disenfranchisement, Democrats would have won every postwar presidential election except 1984. So this is a strange and potentially explosive contradiction: a political system that professes "color blindness" and yet needs race to rule.

The incorporation of opposition via the ideology of color blindness originated during the late 1960s. The idea that we can "get beyond race" when every social scientific indicator available indicates that racial inequality is as endemic as it ever was—this is the key contradiction I am talking about. Yes, racial discrepancies in unemployment, life expectancy, infant mortality, returns to education, arrest and incarceration rates, and above all income and wealth distribution, remain as bad as they ever were; in some respects they have dramatically worsened in recent years. But also the rearticulation of race and racism played a crucial role in this historical reframing. After the 1960s race and racism were reinterpreted as matters of ideas and attitudes, not issues of social structure, economic inequality, power and powerlessness, inclusion and exclusion. Hegemony via the "incorporation of opposition," you see. It's not that there has been no reform; it's not that there has been no racial "progress." It's not that black and brown folk, and Indians, and Asian Americans, and immigrants, have achieved nothing at all. Rather what has happened is that the meaning of race and popular understandings of racism have been regrooved under the banner of color blindness. Today any serious challenge to racism is itself interpreted as racist. This has been a far more effective strategy than old-school "massive resistance" to civil rights movement demands would ever have been. A complete lack of "progress" would not have achieved those hegemonic ends.

All these trends fit into the larger pattern of conflict that has followed the containment by about 1970 of the black movement and the allied movements it generated—brown/red/yellow power, immigrants rights, "second-wave feminism," the antiwar and LGBT movements, and yes, the environmentalist movement too. Sure, resurgent capitalism—or as it is now called, "neoliberalism"—opposed those movements. But it did so by incorporating and thus containing them, rearticulating them as right-wing populist movements with disingenuous labels and "coded" messages. The "right-to-life" movement, "the silent majority," "the Christian coalition," "the tea party," all exemplify this move. So today antiracism activists are attacked for "playing the race card" when they are trying to integrate a school system, trying to get jobs for black or brown people, trying to rebuild the ghetto of Detroit. Just bringing up race is racist now.

Although the color-blind racial regime still exercises a great deal of influence, and poses significant challenges for the democratic and inclusionist legacies that civil rights, black power, and feminism bequeathed to us, the right wing has not won. The radical democratic legacy remains strong, even if we do not have the influence and momentum that we had in, say, 1969. Our movements, our commitments to an expanded democracy and an inclusive society, are growing once again. This is visible especially in electoral politics, where despite a concerted and despotic effort to block it, a coalition of voters of color, women, and young people—and a growing number of whites as well—is trending blue. While the Democrats have not yet forsaken their corporate ties and militarism, they remain far more attentive to voters of color, women, and working people than do the Republicans.

A great political confrontation is looming. It will pit a growing majority of the American people– a designation that is becoming "majority-minority," less and less white—against the 1 percent (or the .1 percent, or the .01 percent). At stake will be state capacity: Will the state at all levels—federal, state, and local—be reduced to a merely repressive apparatus, or will it be able to carry out social provisioning? Will it simply constitute a "monopoly of legitimate violence" (as Max Weber defined it), acting on behalf of the 1 percent, or will it recommit to fulfilling the needs of the American people who elect it and fund it: needs for education, health care, infrastructure, employment, transportation, and so on. And the need for peace, people, the need to end U.S. military intervention around the world.

Will the burgeoning inequality we have seen over the last few decades, and especially since 2008, be meaningfully reduced? So far there is no indication that it will be. In fact, the 1 percent have picked up virtually all the economic benefits produced by the tepid economic recovery that has occurred under Obama: the 99 percent has seen a further net decline of income (of 0.4 percent) under Obama, while the 1 percent has seen an 11.2 percent increase (Saez 2013).

Yet, as the country trends bluer electorally and darker demographically, the confrontation between the emerging political majority and the tenaciously oblivious oligarchs at the top of the stratification pyramid becomes more and more inevitable. Our task now is to mobilize and organize for the coming battle.

REFERENCES

Alexander, Michelle. 2012. *The New Jim Crow: Mass Incarceration in the Age of Colorblindness*, 2nd ed. New York: The New Press.

Manza, Jeff, and Christopher Uggen. 2006. *Locked Out: Felon Disenfranchisement and American Democracy*. New York: Oxford University Press.

Saez, Emmanuel. 2013. "Striking It Richer: The Evolution of Top Incomes in the United States (Updated with 2011 estimates)." University of California, Berkeley Department of Economics, January 23. http://elsa.berkeley.edu/~saez/saez-US-topincomes-2011.pdf.

Chapter Five

America's Struggle with Integration
The Continued Struggle for Its Soul
john powell

"America is continually struggling for its soul."

—Gunnar Myrdal[1]

Although those words were written sixty years ago, they have equal force today. Upon the fiftieth anniversary of the March on Washington and over a half a century since *Brown v. Board of Education*, America remains ambivalent about integration. Since the *Brown* litigation, there has been disagreement about the strategy that would best achieve racial justice. Many parents of children in segregated southern schools simply wanted equal facilities and resources and were ambivalent about pursuing an integration agenda. The NAACP lawyers who litigated the *Brown* cases believed that integration was a necessary condition to equality, and stipulated that tangible resources were equalized or being equalized when they challenged the doctrine of "separate but equal."[2] As a consequence, the *Brown* decision held that segregation is *inherently* unequal.[3] To hold otherwise would be little more than enforcing "separate, but equal."

Yet, the truth that separate is inherently unequal remains as unappreciated as the goal of integration seems elusive. A decade after what Sheryll Cashin described as integration exhaustion,[4] segregation by race and class has grown, especially since the financial crisis.[5] As integration seems ever elusive, many wonder if integration had simply failed. A participant at the Fiftieth Anniversary of the March on Washington for Jobs and Freedom reportedly said, "We wanted equality. We got integration."[6]—while in fact, we got neither integration nor equality. Even my friend the great Derrick Bell, later in life, questioned the merits of a focus on integration: "From the standpoint of education, we would have been better served had the court in *Brown* rejected the petitioners' arguments to overrule *Plessy v. Ferguson*."[7] Professor Bell, perhaps disillusioned with the tepid gains and halting progress, felt that more might have been achieved by enforcing equalization of resources. But if Derrick believed integration was not desirable, he also believed equality was not possible.[8]

Despite lingering ambivalence about the experience of desegregation efforts, we must not lose sight of the enduring truth that a segregated society will never achieve equality or hope that we can pursue it. Indeed, integration remains a good in itself and one of our best strategies to achieve equality. Part of our frustration with integration is the failure to be clear what integration is and is not. We need to distinguish between desegregation and assimilation versus integration.[9] Integration involves ethical and moral dimensions. It is not just material.

Integration is not just what we have or where we live. It is more than facilities, teachers, and resources; it is a project with ontological implications. It should not merely be an instrument that shapes access to equal resources and opportunities. Integration is about who we are and who we will become.

In this chapter, I argue that we must reclaim the goal of integration as a project of national interest. Not only is segregation still inherently unequal, it produces inequality and a society divided against itself. I will explore why integration must be an explicit goal and why further clarity around our conceptions of integration is needed. First, I will examine the most recent data on spatial segregation and ways of understanding and measuring it. Second, I will canvass the ethical and moral dimensions of integration as framed in the works of scholars like Elizabeth Anderson. Finally, I will examine the emerging complexities and suggest reasons to be hopeful that integration may be closer than we think.

SEGREGATION TODAY

Claims of integration have been typed into easily constructed equal opportunity disclaimers, photographed into easily photo-shopped educational and employment brochures, and programmed into easily coded websites that declare commitments to diversity. One has to ask: Are we under a spell? The data and our everyday experiences suggest a different reality. Despite progress well into the 1990s in terms of both desegregation and the reduction of concentrated poverty that is so often a feature of segregation,[10] other trends have either not improved much or have moved decisively in the other direction since.

Historically, and as of 2006, meaningful differences between whites' preference for and comfort with integration continues to differ from blacks'.

Blacks remain willing to live in areas where their group is in the minority and show a clear preference to not live in neighborhoods that are all black.[11] Whites on the other hand, on average, have a stronger preference for same-race neighbors, preferring a neighborhood that is greater than a majority white. Whites typically are three to four times more likely to prefer an entirely same-race neighborhood.[12] Blacks, however, tend to have the weakest preference for living an entirely same-race neighborhood. As expected, housing patterns are measured in ways that go beyond surveys and experiments.

As segregation has become an increasingly important measure of our progress toward equality, a variety of measures have emerged for gauging it. I will briefly survey them. The most popular method is known as the dissimilarity index.[13]

A dissimilarity index shows how unevenly various racial/ethnic groups are spread across neighborhoods within metropolitan areas.[14] A score on this index indicates that the proportion of any particular group is the same across all neighborhoods ("complete integration"); a score of 100 indicates that every neighborhood has residents of only one particular group ("complete segregation").[15] According to the black-white dissimilarity index in 2010, 59 percent of either group would have to move to a different tract for the two groups to become equally distributed.[16] Of these, the ten with the highest levels of segregation include: Detroit; Milwaukee; New York; Newark; Chicago; Philadelphia; Miami; Cleveland; St. Louis; and Nassau-Suffolk, New York.

Because of the limitations[17] of the dissimilarity index, Massey and Denton identify the isolation index as a better measure of exposure to other groups.[18] It goes beyond the limitations inherent in our tendency to only think about or measure how far marginalized U.S. groups tend to live apart from whites. The isolation index allows us to reasonably measure how many underrepresented persons or persons of a particular socioeconomic class are clustered or isolated together. In 1990, and for residential neighborhoods that were majority-black, 38 percent of the residents were poor.[19]

For neighborhoods that were majority Hispanic, 34 percent of the residents were poor.[20] And for neighborhoods that were majority white, only 12 percent of the residents were poor.[21] These figures have largely remained unchanged since 1970, indicating a persistent level of residential segregation that isolates and concentrates poor blacks and Hispanics.

The exposure index is another useful measurement. The exposure index "shows the percentage of residents of one racial-ethnic group who live in the average neighborhood of a designated group."[22] In other words, it measures the amount of interaction between members of a marginalized group and the majority group or with each other. According to Galster's research, "the average black person today lives in a neighborhood with virtually the same percentage of white neighbors (33 percent) as in 1990. Both the average

Hispanic and Asian household lives in a neighborhood with six percentage points fewer whites today than in 1990, due primarily to rapid recent immigration and the fertility rates of these groups."[23]

A fourth measurement for segregation is the "segregation index." The segregation index "uses the difference between the proportion of a particular group in a single sub-area and the proportion of all group members."[24] This index has been found to be particularly useful when studying "changes over time where poverty has increased faster over the last 10 years than the school population."[25]

These indices reflect what many of our experiences have already confirmed: Our residential neighborhoods, workplaces, schools, and pathways to credit, institutional support, and public goods are deeply racialized and racially and socioeconomically segregated. According to the 2006–2009 American Community Survey (ACS), 75 percent of African American families reside in just 16 percent of census tracts.[26] Another indication of this hypersegregation[27] is the fact that 30 percent of African Americans live in Census Block Groups that are 75 percent African American or more.[28] The point here is that residential, racial segregation is as pronounced today as it was at the time of the passage of the Fair Housing Act of 1968.

A corollary to racial segregation is income segregation. Sean Reardon has brilliantly exposed the ways in which our nation is driving toward largely affluent and poor neighborhood clustering.[29] The proportion of families living in poor or affluent neighborhoods doubled from 1970 to 2007, while the proportion of families living in middle-income neighborhoods declined from 65 to 44 percent.[30] Moreover, income segregation among black and Hispanic families grew even *more* rapidly than among non-Hispanic whites since 2000.[31] This has resulted in stark and growing isolation of the poor and extreme poor, who are increasingly racialized on account of their experience of concentrated poverty.

Though researchers cannot say with certainty which factors best explain black and white preferences for neighborhood racial composition, some hypotheses have more evidence than others. Three main hypotheses have been studied: (1) in-group preference or ethnocentrism, (2) race-based neighborhood stereotyping or classism, and (3) racial prejudice.[32] "In-group preference hypothesis (ethnocentrism) argues that all groups have strong desires for neighborhoods with substantial numbers of co-ethnics that reflect a simple, natural ethnocentrism rather than out-group hostility or an effort to preserve relative status advantages."[33] One such example would be the argument that "blacks' own preference for self-segregation explains current levels of black-white segregation."[34] Generally, classism arguments relate to theories that argue preferences are primarily rooted in a desire to avoid residential contact with poor people, and thus undesirable social-class characteristics such as joblessness, welfare dependency, or proclivity to criminal behavior.[35] Without exploring too deeply statistical analyses or the racial prejudice hypothesis, credible research by housing expert Camille Zubrinsky Charles and others has shown that for both blacks and whites, neighborhood racial composition preferences are primarily a function of racial prejudice.[36]

THE ETHICAL IMPERATIVE OF INTEGRATION

Segregation creates a culture of hierarchy and subordination.[37] Segregation can be thought of as a way of hoarding resources for some groups and limiting and excluding them for others. While we most often frame issues of segregation in terms of physical space and the hoarding of material goods, we can also think of segregation as the hoarding of belonging. As I have written before:

> Slavery helped shape the identity and sense of self of all Americans by "rendering blacks all but invisible to those imagining the American community." Segregation under Jim Crow and later embraced in *Plessy* was an extension of the same imagining. The division of membership, of structuring the national community along racial lines is a legacy we struggle with today.[38] .

While many are willing to reference this legacy, or the "stain" that resulted from these eras, many have not linked today's segregation to such arrangements, effects, and hoarding. Segregation and integration are not just about the separation and distribution of material goods or geographic space, but the constitution and distribution of *being*. Segregation, and especially racial residential segregation, shapes the identity and sense of self of all Americans, and it continues to render black and brown people as less than full members to those imagining the American community. This pattern is easy to observe in the context of education, although these structures are intrinsically interconnected. Much of the dynamics of education segregation is maintained through patterns of segregated housing.[39]

According to a 2012 report from The Civil Rights Project, 80 percent of Latino students and 74 percent of black students attend majority nonwhite schools (50–100 percent nonwhite), and 43 percent of Latinos and 38 percent of blacks attend intensely segregated schools (those with only 0–10 percent of white students) across the nation.[40] Fifteen percent of black students, and 14 percent of Latino students, attend "apartheid schools" across the nation, where whites make up 0 to 1 percent of the enrollment.[41] Apartheid schools are even more pervasive in areas with large concentrations of black and brown residents. For example, in Chicago metro, half of the black students attend apartheid schools. In New York, one-third of black students attend such schools.[42] The same is true in the Los Angeles metro, where roughly 30 percent of Latinos attend a school in which whites make up 1 percent or less of the enrollment.[43]

It is important to recognize that these patterns reflect *re-segregation.* "In the West, the share of Latino students in [intensely segregated schools] has increased fourfold, from 12 percent in 1968 to 43 percent in 2009. "In the early 1990s, the average Latino and black student attended a school where roughly a third of students were low income (as measured by free and reduced-price lunch eligibility), but now attend schools where low-income students account for nearly two-thirds of their classmates."

Many would argue that these patterns are not simply the function of law, that such patterns reflect a function of our political culture and social norms. The question is, however, what functions of culture and norms are maintaining segregation and driving re-segregation? Of course, to argue that these patterns are a function of norms ignores the way norms, culture, and law interact. And has there been a serious attempt to overturn Chief Justice Taney's opinion that persons of African descent are "beings of an inferior order, and altogether unfit to associate with the white race"? In answer to this question, the distribution of white students is not encouraging. "Though whites make up just over half of the nation's enrollment, the typical white student attends a school where three-quarters of their peers are white."[44]

As I alluded to in the introduction, integration is not always the response to the widespread, durable, and systemic segregation described above. Instead, calls for the equal distribution of resources, "diversity," and "equity" without disturbing spatial segregation have abounded. These responses, though, are ill-equipped and asymmetrical to segregation's effects, which include group-based stigmatization, deprivation of citizenship, categorical inequality, and the severing of groups from the imagined American (and, as the mind sciences demonstrate, the human) community. As suggested earlier, segregation in marking who belongs and who does not also helps to constitute the meaning and identity of those inside and those marginalized. This is the "stigma" that *Brown* was trying to address and Professor Charles Lawrence elaborated on.[45] More broadly, it is social death that not fully belonging leads to, that integration is situated to address—the "deepest degradation" that Chief Justice Taney asserted permanently "fixed upon [a] whole race."[46] Further, neither diversity nor separate-but-equal mitigates for "the fact that blacks live several years less than whites, that 13 percent of black men are disenfranchised due to a felony conviction, and that more than one-third of black [and Latino] children live in poverty."[47]

There is also the mistaken belief by many that integration is assimilation. Minority groups are brought into the tent but only if they mimic the already dominant group. The composition of the group may change but everything else remains the same. As an aspirational and empirical matter, this is highly contestable. It is more likely and probably more desirable that as groups engage and interact the values and norms of both groups will change, and the lines of differentiation between groups will also be redrawn. Integration, then, is not just joining some existing order but having a chance to help constitute a new emerging order as well.

As Elizabeth Anderson notes in *The Imperative of Integration*, integration responds to the "persistence of large, systemic, and seemingly intractable disadvantages that track lines of group identity, along with troubling patterns of intergroup interaction that call into question our claim to be a fully democratic society of equal citizens."[48] Integration limits opportunity hoarding,[49] uneven levels of group leverage,[50] stereotyping, and prejudice; it accounts for or limits exploitation, marginalization, group-based violence,[51] cultural imperialism, and powerlessness[52] and it limits intergroup interaction that only or usually occurs when it is "based on relations of domination and exploitation."[53]

Integration responds to Anderson's concerns, and much more. Integration responds to our tendency to place social, spiritual, and structural walls between ourselves and underserved "others." It is transformative, revealing that there is more at stake than the material and nonmaterial. Integration *is* a spiritual and moral project that goes beyond re-creating boundaries.[54] It re-creates beings.

The back-and-forth nature of our legal institutions, strategies, and willingness to try to get it right, reflect our discomfort with shared vulnerability and interdependence. We construct exclusive structures, neighborhoods, and zoning laws, only to turn around and hope that we are empathetic and supportive of each other in times of unavoidable crisis or interdependency. These approaches largely reflect inadequate understandings of and commitments to who we think we are and to what shapes who we are.

Integration moves us away from the illusion that we are separate and unconnected. In doing so, we move away from not just sorting people in physical and social space, but also in psychic space, the imagined community of that space.[55] In such spaces, boundaries and sorting regulate who can and cannot become a member, as well as who can and cannot access opportunity. In *Brown*, a unanimous court recognized this dynamic in its discussion of segregation and stigmatization. In that case, the harm was not merely about resources not being equal. The harm was that "separate" was inherently unequal. As our understandings continue to develop, it has become increasingly clear that "separate" stratifies groups' well-being, citizenship, and access to opportunity. The stratified existence that migrates with blacks, almost regardless of their income, on issues related to housing, political representation, access to credit, employment, institutional investment, vigilante justice, and the criminal justice system are all related to blacks' location within structures and psyches. In the social and cognitive spheres, blacks are often the "out-group," with stigmatization and segregation operating as catalysts.[56]

Integration relocates the "out-group" (which often is, but does not have to be, a racialized group). As Douglas S. Massey documented, "When members of an out-group are well integrated spatially, stratification is more difficult and costly because divestment in the out-group must occur on a person-by-person, family-by-family basis."[57] To the contrary, "whenever the powerful have sought to stigmatize and subordinate a particular social group, they have endeavored to confine its members to specific neighborhoods by law, edict, or practice."[58]

Herein lies a dilemma: too few Americans can be convinced that, here in the United States, the "powerful" are seeking to "stigmatize and subordinate a particular group," and yet particular groups continue to be stigmatized and subordinated, so much that many of them are no longer perceived to be human at the unconscious level. Many Americans view explicit and overt attempts to stigmatize and subordinate groups as objectionable, offensive, and morally inexcusable. And yet, there are many whose words and actions suggest that they believe certain groups are not capable of developing into worthy students, neighbors, workers, parents, or citizens. This reality is nothing like Dr. King's dream. Worse, for a nation that invokes justice, love, freedom, equality, fairness, and opportunity, we create and accept structured spaces that yield the opposite. We create and accept structured spaces that yield what Massey calls "durable inequality, a structured state wherein stratification replicates and reproduces itself more or less automatically over time."[59] When a nation has categorical and group inequality that is systemic, widespread, and durable—as is the case in the United States—inaction is beyond inadequate. It is morally inexcusable.

We have to decide: stratification or transformation. We are in need of a new way of being and new ways of shaping who we are. Integration, which is not to be confused with assimilation, transforms spaces—be it physical structures (e.g., residential areas) or our individual and collective psyche (e.g., implicit and unconscious thoughts). Indeed, integration transforms all and would transform much. At stake is whether we are going to hold tightly to the belief that separation and stratification are normal or natural—and, whether we are going to continue denying membership and access to opportunity to those who, if engaged in integrated spaces, would be perceived to be just like us and a part of us.

EMERGING COMPLEXITIES

Changing Demographics

"Dramatic increases in residential integration," according to Jay Readey, "are coming faster than anyone thinks."[60] In fact, Readey predicts that the black-white dissimilarity indices in America's most segregated metropolitan areas will all drop below 50. Though a contrary opinion appears below, Readey believes the dissimilarity index should always be the "measuring stick" for integration. Moreover, Readey believes the United States is quickly approaching a tipping point[61]—one caused by increases in intermarriage[62] and biracial children. Citing The Pew Research Center's data, which found that 15 percent of all marriages were intermarriage in 2010, Readey argues that a steady increase in intermarriages will dramatically increase the "demand for stable, racially and culturally mixed neighborhoods." Readey's reasoning and prediction is encouraging, but there are nuances that require further examination.

Asian and Latino populations, as we know, are growing. If all of our institutions (and the decision makers within them) were half white and Asian or half black and Latino, would we call these institutions or such spaces integrated? Many of us would respond with "no" or "probably not." In this example, we would likely recognize that such a conception of integration would be narrow, and perhaps would marginalize and redefine others' status and their well-being—namely their citizenship and the degree to which they belong. So, we must be clear, what is "true integration"?

In the context of education, "integration is the systemic transformation of a school to create a diverse and inclusive environment within the school and the curricula. . . . [I]ntegration is not simply a goal in terms of the schools in which students learn as a static site, but requires a transformation of the setting in which the identities of students are formed and form others," which is consistent with the principal goals of education: the "creation of an effective citizenry and the opening of a space for a truly multi-racial, multi-ethnic society."[63]

We cannot and should not assume that a shift in demographics will automatically create an effective citizenry or such a space. The attack on ethnic studies in Texas and the Voting Rights Act of 1965, and the proliferation of Voter ID laws are illustrative.[64] Developments in the South are also illuminating. In a 2012 report, researchers determined that "the share of Latino students attending intensely segregated minority schools has increased steadily over the past four decades from 33.7 percent in 1968 to 43.1 percent in 2009, [where] presently more than two out of five Latino students in the South attend intensely segregated settings." In Atlanta, "as their share of enrollment has grown, Latino exposure to whites has fallen substantially—by nearly ten percentage points since 2002."[65]

Yet, even if a shift in demographics leads others to embrace some traditionally marginalized groups more, this cannot be taken to prove that integration has arrived or that integration itself is the goal. For example, "In ten Southern metros, the typical Latino attends a school where at least 40 percent of students are white. By comparison, only in the Raleigh metro did black students experience similarly high levels of exposure to white students."[66] Certainly we see evidence of varying levels of racial bias also with Asians, for the degree in which they are embraced is still tied to considerations related to opportunity hoarding and racial hierarchies.[67]

In addition, shifts in demographics might lead us to rethink which measures of segregation and which integration goals best reflect the most important trends. As Richard Rothstein observed in 2012, multiple reports have recently celebrated "the end of segregation" and its "decline." In celebrating a drop in the black dissimilarity index, these researchers seemingly failed to account for the increase in low-income Latino and Asian immigration into black neighborhoods. Moving forward, as Rothstein suggests, the exposure of black Americans to white Americans might be a better measurement. Using this index, it becomes easier to identify increases in high-poverty neighborhoods,[68] a key driving force and product of segregation.

If nothing else, pre-celebrations of the end of segregation should remind us of the need to remain flexible in our strategies and diligent in our efforts to identify new arrangements that could advance racial justice.

The Black Middle Class

Segregation is not just about segregating people based on a trait. Segregation is also about the distribution of opportunity and identity. Increasingly, middle-class black Americans are accepting this reality and are responding to it by moving to neighborhoods that are suburban, not predominantly black, or both. For such black Americans, the lure of suburbia and non-black communities is largely the same. They are looking to escape concentrated black poverty and the effects and meanings that attach to persons trapped there.

Sheryll Cashin, in *The Failures of Integration: How Race and Class Are Undermining the American Dream*, explored this complexity. When an Ivy League–educated, senior executive of a media company was questioned about why he and his family lived where they do, he spoke to the link between opportunity and segregation: "If our number one criteria had been [public] school quality, in reality we would have ended up in a white area."[69] For many black Americans, and no different than many nonblack Americans, school quality is the deciding factor when deciding where to live.[70] This is a familiar U.S. dynamic. Segregation suffocates opportunity, and black bodies are, once again, attempting to flee areas that bear strange fruit.[71] To drive the point, where would middle-class blacks choose to live, or any group for the matter, if their number one priority was quality and accessible supermarkets? Banking institutions? Lending institutions? Recreational facilities? Parks? Health facilities? Museums? Government services? Low teacher-to-student ratios? Mentors? Increasing property values? Responsive law enforcement? Investment by growing employment industries? Political representation?[72] Would any of these considerations lead you to choose a predominantly black city? What is more, not only does black middle-class flight reflect residential isolation and destabilization, it creates and reinforces it. For many Americans, and especially black, brown, and poor, the middle class is getting an increasingly smaller peace of the pie.

In his 2011 article, "Growth in the Residential Segregation of Families by Income, 1970–2009," Sean F. Reardon researched changes in family income segregation patterns in 117 metropolitan areas, with a particular focus on changes since 2000.[73] In tracking increasingly unequal and separate residential realities, Reardon identified the following major findings:

- In 1970 only 15 percent of families were in neighborhoods that we classify as either affluent (neighborhoods where median incomes were greater than 150 percent of median income in their metropolitan areas) or poor (neighborhoods where median incomes were less than 67 percent of metropolitan median income). By 2007, 31 percent of families lived in such neighborhoods.
- Income segregation among black and Hispanic families increased much more than did income segregation among white families from 1970 to 2007. Notably, income segregation among black and Hispanic families grew very sharply from 2000 to 2007. Income segregation among black and Hispanic families is now much higher than among white families.

As Reardon points out, there is a growing decline in the proportion of families in middle-class neighborhoods. Though this is true for all families, this is most true for black families, with income segregation growing four times as much as whites between 1970 and 2007.[74] More recently, income segregation among blacks grew even faster between 2000 and 2007, a period that largely predates the most recent financial crisis. These trends are consistent with Hispanic residential patterns, though not as stark. Though there are multiple ways to calculate income segregation, the research appears to lead to the same conclusion: isolation is increasing among high-income and low-income families and middle-income neighborhoods are declining. It almost seems too obvious to state that the life chances for low-income blacks are not moving in the right direction.

As I said previously, segregation distributes identity. To some degree, middle-class blacks have accepted identities that segregation has constructed around low-income blacks. Prince George's County, Maryland, the highest income majority-black county in the United States has seen its residents and officials take efforts to keep low-income blacks from their ranks.[75] Still, Prince George's County "typically ranks second worst in the state of Maryland on test scores, after Baltimore, a predominantly black and heavily poor city."[76] Graduation rates are also disproportionately low. Similar to segregated lower-class neighborhoods, wealth disparities track black middle-class residents, and a sizable number of parents who can afford to either provide homeschooling or send their children to private school often do. As one parent noted, "I would love the idea of being able to send my daughters to public school, but not the way most of them are now. . . . If you don't get into a good magnet program, you're sending your children to a school with uncertified teachers, not enough books, large number of children who don't behave."[77]

Here, the identity of segregated inner-city public schools and students is not too dissimilar from public schools and students in black middle-class neighborhoods. The identity segregation imposes cannot easily be escaped. This pattern of identity migration and stigmatization is found in other areas of black middle-class neighborhoods: statistics around police shootings of unarmed blacks, the steering of jobs and economic growth away from black neighborhoods, worse government services, disproportionately low commercial investment, fewer restaurants, a decreasing tax base, etc. Ultimately, whether it is a segregated low-income community or a segregated middle-class community, blacks' identities are largely shaped by the former. This is not lost on Cashin: "Painfully, I have come to the conclusion that external prejudice against black neighborhoods makes it virtually impossible for the black middle class to form havens of their own that approximate the economic or opportunity benefits of a white enclave. . . . Most black suburban movers will find that the social distress they sought to escape has migrated to them."[78]

CONCLUSION

I have called myself a radical integrationist. The world is getting smaller and people are migrating and interacting as never before. New identities are being born and boundaries are shifting. Yet, many oppose in practice, if not in law, integration, and the law has been too willing to naturalize this practice and protect it. That must be challenged. But that is not my point here. Those of us who are integrationists sometimes are unwilling to accept that fear of integration, and confront the corollary anxiety around growing diversity that reflects a morally deficient individual and society. I believe this is a mistake. While the sense of self may be very elastic over time, it is stable in the short-run.

Those of us who support integration must find new ways to support it without shutting down those who express, through practice or word, the fear of losing their community and self through integration. I believe we must make space for such fears to be constructively expressed and for a positive vision of a difference space and emerging self. This push must occur at multiple levels, from the neighborhood to the nation as a whole. We must continue to redraw boundaries until none are outside, knowing that it will change what those boundaries mean and who we are inside. This is a project that must be part and parcel with our continued push for integration.

If we reclaim the goal of integration as a project of national interest and make it an explicit goal, new structures and ways of being will be formed. In addition to marching for equality, and coming together to celebrate those who did, we should march toward equality. If and when integration becomes central to that march, there will still be struggle, but there will be much less exhaustion.

NOTES

1. Gunnar Myrdal, *An American Dilemma: The Negro Problem and Modern Democracy* (New York: Harper Brothers Publishers, 1944).

2. Brown v. Board of Education Topeka, 347 U.S. 483, 492, 74 S. Ct. 686 (1954).

3. Ibid. at 49 ("We conclude that, in the field of public education, the doctrine of 'separate but equal' has no place. Separate educational facilities are inherently unequal. Therefore, we hold that the plaintiffs and others similarly situated for whom the actions have been brought are, by reason of the segregation complained of, deprived of the equal protection of the laws guaranteed by the Fourteenth Amendment.").

4. Sheryll Cashin, *The Failures of Integration: How Race and Class Are Undermining the American Dream* (New York: Public Affairs, 2004).

5. Paul Jargowsky and Todd Swanstrom, *City Vitals Series: Economic Integration: Why It Matters and How Cities Can Get More of It*, CEOs for Cities, p.1, retrieved from http://www.ceosforcities.org/pagefiles/EconomicIntegration.pdf.

6. Michelle Norris, "One Dream," *Time*, August 26, 2013.

7. Lisa Trei, "Black Children Might Have Been Better Off without *Brown v. Board*, Bell Says," *Stanford Report*, April 21, 2004, retrieved from http://news.stanford.edu/news/2004/april21/brownbell-421.html; Plessy v. Ferguson, 163 U.S. 537 (1896).

8. Ibid.

9. Trayvon Martin was killed in a desegregated community, but was it integrated? Similarly, is a desegregated public school that has dual tracking and that puts whites on one curriculum (i.e., advanced courses) and blacks on another integrated?

10. P. A. Jargowsky, *Stunning Progress, Hidden Problems: The Dramatic Decline of Concentrated Poverty in the 1990s*. Living Cities Census Series 1, Center on Urban and Metropolitan Policy (Washington, DC: The Brookings Institution), 6–13, retrieved from http://www.brookings.edu/~/media/research/files/reports/2003/5/demographics%20jargowsky/jargowskypoverty.pdf

11. C. Z. Charles, "Who Will Live Near Whom?" Poverty & Race Research Action Council (September/October 2008), retrieved from http://www.prrac.org/full_text.php?text_id=1190&item_id=11272&newsletter_id=101&header=Race+%2F+Racism&kc=1.

12. Ibid.

13. For advantages and disadvantages: see S. Gorard and C. Taylor, "What Is Segregation? A Comparison of Measures in Terms of Strong and Weak Compositional Invariance," *Sociology* 36 (2002).

14. G. Galster, "Urban Opportunity Structure and Racial/Ethnic Polarization," Wayne State University, College of Urban, Labor, and Metropolitan Affairs, 2005, 1–26, retrieved from http://www.clas.wayne.edu/Multimedia/DUSP/files/land_use_db/Opportunity_Structure.pdf; see also G. Galster and Jackie Gutsinger, "Racial Settlement and Metropolitan Land Use and Patterns: Does Sprawl Abet Black-White Segregation?" *Urban Geography* 28, no. 6 Jackie (2007): 516–53.

15. Galster, "Urban Opportunity Structure," 5.

16. John R. Logan and Brian Stults, "The Persistence of Segregation in the Metropolis: New Findings from the 2010 Census," Census Brief prepared for U.S. 2010 (2011).

17. See, for example, L. M. Quinn, *Assumptions and Limitations of the Census Bureau Methodology Ranking Racial and Ethnic Residential Segregation in Cities and Metro Areas* (Milwaukee: University of Wisconsin–Milwaukee Employment and Training Institute, 2004).

18. Douglas Massey and Nancy Denton, *American Apartheid* (Cambridge, MA: Harvard University Press, 1993).

19. Galster, "Urban Opportunity Structure," 6.

20. Ibid.

21. Ibid.

22. Ibid.; W. F. Tate IV, *Research on Schools, Neighborhoods and Communities: Toward Civic Responsibility*, The American Educational Research Association (Lanham, MD: Rowman & Littlefield, 2012), 53.

23. Galster, "Urban Opportunity Structure," 6.

24. C. Taylor, S. Gorard, and S. Fitz, "A Re-examination of Segregation Indices in Terms of Compositional Invariance," *Social Research Update* 30 (2000); see S. Gorard, *Education and Social Justice* (Cardiff: University of Wales Press); S. Gorard and C. Taylor, "What Is Segregation? A Comparison of Measures in Terms of 'Strong' and 'Weak' Compositional Invariance," *Sociology* 36, no. 4 (2002) 875–96.

25. Taylor Gorard, and Fitz, "A Re-examination of Segregation Indices."

26. See M. Brenman and T. W. Sanchez, *Planning as if People Matter: Governing for Equity* (Washington, DC: Island Press, 2012), 31; see also Equal Justice Society and Wilson Sonsini Goodrich & Rosati, "Lessons from *Mt. Holly*: Leading Scholars Demonstrate Need for Disparate Impact Standard to Combat Implicit Bias," *Hastings Race and Poverty Law Journal* (Summer 2004): 247, retrieved from https://www.wsgr.com/attorneys/BIOS/PDFs/berger-0614.pdf.; Craig Gurian, "Mapping and Analysis of New Data Documents Still-Segregated America," *Remapping Debate* (January 18, 2011), retrieved from http://tinyurl.com/4ac3k5z. Census tracks are subdivisions of a county. They usually have between 2,500 and 8,000 persons and are intended to approximate neighborhoods. See www.census.gov/geo/www/cen_tract.html.

27. Massey and Denton defined hypersegregation as extreme segregation across five dimensions: evenness, exposure, clustering, centralization, and concentration. See D. S. Massey and N. A. Denton, "Hypersegregration in U.S. Metropolitan Areas: Black and Hispanic Segregation along Five Dimensions," *Demography* 26, no. 3 (1989), 376–91 (arguing blacks experience hypersegregration at levels not experienced by other racial groups).

28. Brenman and Sanchez, *Planning as if People Matter*, 31.

29. S. F. Reardon and K. Bischoff, *Growth in the Residential Segregation of Families by Income, 1970–2009*, US2010 Project (2011), 1, 8, retrieved from http://www.s4.brown.edu/us2010/Data/Report/report111111.pdf.

30. Ibid., 21.

31. Ibid.

32. L. Bobo and C. Zubrinsky, "Attitudes on Residential Integration: Perceived Status Differences, Mere In-Group Preference, or Racial Prejudice?" *Social Forces* 74, no. 3 (1996): 883–909, retrieved from http://www.wjh.harvard.edu/soc/faculty/bobo/pdf%20documents/AttRes.pdf.

33. C. Z. Charles, "The Dynamics of Racial Residential Segregation," *Annual Review of Sociology* 29 (2003): 167, 182; see W. A. V. Clark, "Residential Preferences and Residential Choices in a Multiethnic Context," *Demography* 29, no. 3 (1992): 451.

34. See Charles, "The Dynamics of Racial Residential Segregation," 182.

35. See, e.g., B. Whitley and M. Kite, *The Psychology of Prejudice and Discrimination* (Boston: Cengage Learning, 2009), 23.

36. See, e.g., Charles, "The Dynamics of Racial Residential Segregation,"182–207.

37. See, e.g., j. a. powell, "Socioeconomic School Integration—A Response," Poverty & Race Research Action Council (November–December 2001), retrieved from http://www.prrac.org/full_text.php?text_id=738&item_id=7780&newsletter_id=59&header=Symposium:%20Socio economic%20School%20Integration.

38. john a. powell and S. Menendian, "Little Rock and the Legacy of Dred Scott," *St. Louis University Law Journal* 52 (December 1, 2008): 1153, 1164.

39. A study of 960 school districts found that cities that implemented metropolitan-wide desegregation plans experienced substantially increased housing integration, an effect evident in districts of all sizes and in all regions of the country.

Districts that have experienced desegregation over the longest period of time have the lowest levels of housing segregation as well. School desegregation between 1968 and 1973 doubled the rate of housing integration in twenty-five central cities with an African American population of at least 100,000. See john a. powell, "Opportunity-Based Housing," *Journal of Affordable Housing & Community Development Law* 12 (2002–2003): 188, 214.

40. Gary Orfield, John Kucesar, and Genevieve Siegel-Hawley, *E Pluribus . . . Separation: Deepening Double Segregation for More Students* (Los Angeles: UCLA/ Civil Rights Project/Proyecto Derechos Civiles, 2012), http://civilrightsproject.ucla. edu/research/k-12-education/integration-and-diversity/mlk-national/e- pluribus...sep-aration-deepening-double-segregation-for-more-students.

41. Ibid.

42. Ibid.

43. Ibid.

44. Ibid.

45. Charles R. Lawrence III, "The Id, the Ego, and Equal Protection: Reckoning with Unconscious Racism," *Stanford Law Review* 39, no. 2 (1987): 317–88.

46. A. Leon Higginbotham Jr., "The Politics of Inferiority," In *Shades of Freedom: Racial Politics and Presumptions of the American Legal Process* (New York: Oxford University Press, 1996), 66.

47. Elizabeth Anderson, "Segregation and Social Inequality," in *The Imperative of Integration* (Princeton, NJ: Princeton University Press, 2010), 2.

48. Ibid.

49. Ibid., 8

50. Ibid., 16

51. Kai Wright, "Life Cycles of Inequity: A Colorlines Series on Black Men," *Colorlines*, http://colorlines.com/archives/2014/05/life_cycles_of_inequity_a_color-lines_series_on_black_men.html (accessed September 12, 2014).

52. Joseph E. Stiglitz, *The Price of Inequality: How Today's Divided Society Endangers Our Future* (New York: W.W. Norton & Co., 2012).

53. Anderson, *The Imperative of Integration*, 15.

54. john a. powell, *Racing to Justice: Transforming Our Conceptions of Self and Other to Build an Inclusive Society.* Bloomington: Indiana University Press, 2012.

55. Ibid.

56. Douglas S. Massey, *Categorically Unequal: The American Stratification System* (New York: Russell Sage Foundation, 2007), 18.

57. Ibid., 19.

58. Ibid.

59. Ibid.

60. Jay S. Readey, *The Coming Integration* (Chicago: Chicago Lawyers' Committee for Civil Rights Under Law, 2013), 2.

61. Malcolm Gladwell, *The Tipping Point: How Little Things Can Make A Big Difference* (New York: Little Brown, 2000).

62. Readey describes intermarriages as marriages of Hispanics and nonwhites with non-Hispanic whites or others.

63. john a. powell, "The Tensions between Integration and School Reform," *Hastings Constitutional Law Quarterly* 28 (2000): 655.

64. See *Shelby County v. Holder*, 570 U.S.__(2013).

65. Genevieve Siegel-Hawley and Erica Frankenberg, "Southern Slippage: Growing School Segregation in the Most Desegregated Region of the Country," The Civil Rights Project, eScholarship, retrieved September 15, 2014, from http://escholarship. org/uc/item/6kb414vh.

66. Ibid.

67. Annie Paul, "It's Not Me, It's You," *New York Times*, October 7, 2012, retrieved September 15, 2014, from http://www.nytimes.com/2012/10/07/opinion/sunday/intelligence-and-the-stereotype-threat.html?_r=0.

68. The Joint Center for Political and Economic Studies defines a "high poverty" neighborhood as one where 30 percent or more of the residents have incomes below the poverty line, but this definition can be misleading: The poverty line is very low, and neighborhoods with poverty rates of greater than 30 percent also inevitably house large numbers of residents whose incomes are barely above the poverty line, and whom most would also consider to be severely economically disadvantaged.

69. Cashin, *The Failures of Integration*, 130.

70. This truth seems to be lost on those who insist that poor families and blacks irresponsibly bought "too much house" and should share blame for the most recent housing crisis.

71. "Tanya McDowell, Homeless Woman, Arrested for Sending Son to School Using Babysitter's Address," *Huffington Post*, April 18, 2011, retrieved from http://www.huffingtonpost.com/2011/04/18/tanya-mcdowell-homeless-w_n_850571.html. ("This now sends a message to other parents that may have been living in other towns and registering their kids with phony addresses.")

72. Stiglitz, *The Price of Inequality*.

73. Sean F. Reardon and Kendra Bischoff, *Growth in the Residential Segregation of Families by Income, 1970–2009*, Advisory Board of the US2010 Project 1 (2011): 1–32, retrieved from http://www.s4.brown.edu/us2010/Data/Report/report111111.pdf.

74. Ibid.

75. In 1994, Prince George's first black county executive campaigned on the assertion that housing was becoming too accessible to low-income D.C. families and successfully sought a release from a court-ordered school busing program that brought in poor students. In 1996, residents hired a private security company to screen nonresidents.

76. Cashin, *The Failures of Integration*, 141.

77. Avis Thomas-Lester, "Fleeing Residents Cite County's Shortcomings," *Washington Post*, June 21, 2001.

78. Sheryll Cashin, "Dilemma of Place and Suburbanization of the Black Middle Class," in *The Black Metropolis in the Twenty-First Century: Race, Power, and Politics of Place*, ed. Robert D. Bullard (Lanham, MD: Rowman & Littlefield, 2007), 89; Monica Potts, "The Collapse of Black Wealth," *American Prospect*, November 21, 2012, retrieved September 15, 2014, from http://prospect.org/article/collapse-black-wealth.

Chapter Six

Moving Beyond Race Fatigue

Challenging Hidden Bias, Getting Serious about Our Racial Future

Andrew Grant Thomas

A great many Americans can appreciate the civil rights leader Fannie Lou Hamer's famous line about being "sick and tired of being sick and tired." That's how we often feel about race. We could not feel otherwise: 2013 is not 1955, much less 1855. The presidency of Barack Obama may not mean the end of race, any more than the abolition of slavery or the death of Jim Crow meant the end of race. But surely the fact that voters, many of them white, twice opted to place a black man in the White House, along with the growing frequency of people of color in positions of leadership in sports and entertainment, politics and business, reflects a genuine opening up of the racial opportunity structure in the United States.

Barack and Michelle Obama, Oprah Winfrey, Nelson Mandela, the Dalai Lama, Condoleezza Rice, Aung San Suu Kyi—every year, people of color feature prominently on the Gallup Poll's list of most admired people. When it comes to race in America, do we really need to keep talking?

I want to offer two reasons why the answer to that question remains an unqualified yes. The first is that talking about race, and specifically about one's own racial bias, is an indispensable step toward mitigating its noxious effects. The second reason is that if we do not talk in concrete and compelling terms about our racial aspirations, we undermine the likelihood of realizing them. The crucial caveat, in both cases, is that talking constructively about race is hard and we have much to learn about how to do it.

THE PERILS OF OUR HIDDEN RACIAL BIASES

Job resumes bearing names associated with whites, such as Emily or Greg, are called back by prospective employers 50 percent more often than identical resumes bearing names associated with black Americans, like Lakisha or Jamal. In video simulations, police officers are more likely to shoot unarmed blacks than unarmed whites, and to shoot armed blacks but not armed whites. A teenager hacks at the lock of a bicycle chained to a post in a public park. When the teen is a white male, an occasional onlooker asks whether the bicycle is his. When the teen is a black male, passersby quickly surround him and take his photograph; some call 911. When the teen is white and female, several people offer to help free "her" bicycle.

Are these employers, police officers, and bystanders racists? Not necessarily—at least, not in the explicit, Archie Bunker-ish way we usually mean by the term. Neuroscientists now know that the origins of most human perception, decision making, and action largely lie outside our conscious awareness or control. It could not be otherwise. Our brains engage some two thousand bits of sensory information every second, only a tiny fraction of which is processed consciously by the prefrontal context or "thinking brain." The rest is routed to the unconscious or "reactive brain," often shaping our judgments and actions in ways hidden to us.

The way our brains process information means that a great deal of our engagement with race, yours and mine, takes place in a cognitive "blind spot." Three-quarters or more of us harbor hidden biases against black Americans relative to white Americans. Whatever our conscious beliefs and values, virtually all of us unwittingly subscribe to one or more racial stereotypes— the assumed foreignness of Latinos, the superior math and science abilities of Asian Americans, or the criminality of African Americans, for example. Hidden biases fuel discriminatory actions. They have been shown to help predict racially inflected sentencing decisions, hiring and salary decisions, medical treatment decisions, verbal and physical abuse of racial others, and much more.

What if we knew that many people in the United States, especially members of its white majority, held biases, often unknown to them, against people of color and especially against black Americans? What if we knew that these biases can lead to discriminatory behaviors? What if we recognized the enormous role that human discretion plays in the distribution of burdens and opportunities in our lives? And what if we recognized that white Americans continue to hold the lion's share of this distributive power?

Under this set of assumptions, the Institute of Medicine's conclusion in 2002 that massive racial disparities in health owed partly to bias by health care providers does not shock us. That blacks and Latinos comprise three in ten members of the nation's general population but seven in ten members of our prison population does not surprise us. Under these circumstances, the failure to direct significant national resources to the distressingly poor and under-resourced schools in which so many children of color languish makes a sad, perverse kind of sense.

My point is not that interpersonal bias accounts for racial inequities. Racial differences in health outcomes are not simply about physician bias, any more than the small number of nonwhite, U.S.-born graduate students in STEM disciplines can be traced only to the cognitive blind spots of graduate admissions officers. The deep, cumulative, institutionally driven advantages and disadvantages that fuel racial gaps in health and educational outcomes are a key part of the diagnosis—and beyond the scope of this chapter. Hidden bias does not tell the whole story of racial inequality, but it has much to say. What, if anything, can we do about it?

OPENING UP ABOUT OUR HIDDEN BIAS

We know more about the pervasiveness and influence of hidden racial bias than about how to mitigate or eliminate its effects. The common thread to the remedial principles and practices we have is to take these biases and stereotypes out of the shadows and expose them to the more deliberate, often generous light of our thinking brain. It also helps if we are genuinely concerned about the presence and effects of bias on our thinking and our behavior. With training, for example, police officers, judges, test subjects, and others have been able to counter the effects of their biases, especially when motivated to do so. Not talking about race leaves hidden biases free to do their corrosive work.

Patricia Devine, a psychologist at the University of Wisconsin–Madison, and an expert on implicit bias, has proposed five strategies for overcoming bias: perspective taking, counter-stereotypic imaging, increasing opportunities for contact, individuation, and stereotype replacement. Each strategy is likely to become more effective if the person using them commits to being as alert as possible to expressions of his own bias and to practicing the strategy. Here, for the sake of space, I elaborate on only the first three.

By perspective taking, Devine means trying actively to adopt another person's perspective on a situation or issue. It is a skill many of us who are parents try to inculcate in our children as the basis of empathy, but often do not practice ourselves. How would it feel to be the one nonwhite person at a social gathering and asked to speak for the group to which I belong? Or to have my racial or ethnic identity dismissed by someone who insists that she doesn't "see" race? Taking the perspective of a racial other can prevent the activation of bias in the first place.

Assuming the other person's perspective after we have acted in a biased way can help us understand her reaction and formulate an empathetic response of our own.

Counter-stereotypic imaging means calling to mind members of the group that disconfirm the stereotype I have. For example, having realized that I just made an unfounded assumption about the nationality of an "Asian"-identified person sitting across the room, I might think of well-known Asian Americans (Michael Chang, Michelle Kwan, Yo-Yo Ma) or of Asian American friends and acquaintances. Some researchers suggest that creating physical environments that showcase positive, counter-stereotypic examples of the groups—hanging photos or posters of Barack Obama, Sonia Sotomayor, and Cesar Chavez on my office wall, say—over time can consistently weaken my unconscious biases against those groups.

Finally, increasing opportunities for contact refers specifically to searching out settings (events, clubs, places of worship) where I am likely to have good interactions with non-stereotypic members of the group in question. More than fifty years ago, psychologist Gordon Allport suggested that the conditions that best support positive contact between groups include having people of equal status, with shared goals, interacting cooperatively rather than competitively, with the support of the law or authority figures. Even at a time of increasing racial and ethnic diversity in the United States, the tendency of Whites to interact and network with other Whites means that, for them, meeting this challenge can require a lot of initiative. Devine suggests that even virtual contact, through movies, television shows, and so on, can be helpful.

It is easy to predict that over the coming years we will learn much more than we now know about hidden bias and how to reduce it. Even then, our work will not be done. In part, that is because while unconscious bias deepens many inequalities, once embedded in our school systems, workplaces, laws, and cultural common sense it may not be needed to sustain them. Making significant progress in remedying racial injustice and inequality will require a multiple approach that speaks to matters of bias, culture, power, and institutional inequities. In my view, making real progress on race will also require hard conversations about what "real progress on race" might look like. Those are conversations we have hardly begun.

ENVISIONING THE RACIAL FUTURE WE WANT

The year is 2042. Surely and dramatically, the racial landscape of the United States has changed over the course of the century. The long-forecast end of the United States as a white-majority country in that year may or may not be a big part of the story. Race still matters, but operates now more to unify than divide us. Many trace the change to the Obama era that ended a quarter-century earlier—not necessarily because of any big new federal policies implemented during that president's time in office, but because of other social and institutional developments that took seed or began to flower then. Some social justice old timers recall that they wept when Obama, our first nonwhite president, took office. They did not know that more meaningful developments were just ahead.

What would a United States another giant step or two toward racial equality and justice look like? What specific and notable markers of racial change would we see, hear, and feel? If promising seeds of change are in place right now, or around the corner, how can we recognize them? How do we move from here to there? Who has what role to play in that movement?

This is the kind of scenario we rarely play out and these are questions we rarely ask ourselves, much less try to answer. Those of us actively working to promote racial justice in the United States almost never develop more than fragmentary visions of what transformative rather than incremental change might look like. This must change. Polls, focus groups, and everyday conversations with friends, family, acquaintances, and strangers confirm that most Americans believe we already have arrived as an enlightened nation on matters of race and ethnicity. If we cannot articulate a positive vision of a racial future distinct from and preferable to our racial present, how can we expect fence-sitters and skeptics to embrace the struggle—and perhaps the sacrifice—required to get there?

Moreover, how can we formulate appropriate strategies without a clear vision of what we mean to achieve and some understanding of how our visions may diverge? You and I may both see the huge number of African Americans and Latinos in U.S. prisons as an indictment of our justice system. However, if my preferred future calls for smaller, but proportional numbers of blacks and Latinos within prisons, while yours calls for the abolition of prisons, we need to talk. But first we must think ahead and compare notes on our thinking. This is very practical work.

Envisioning the future we want is harder than it might first appear. Our initial, naive efforts at envisioning are likely to produce only thinly veiled versions of the present. For example, few of us will think to account in non-trivial ways for the influence of the big social, demographic, technological, and economic drivers that would shape all possible futures—global warming; global migration patterns; advances in biomedical, communications, and transportation technologies; the likely economic ascendancy of India and China and relative decline of the United States; and so on. Even if we do think to account for such factors, not many of us would know how to do so.

In the particular context of race in the United States, two other glitches in our thinking deserve mention and attention. First, we tend to assume the inevitability of racial progress. Nowadays, that general tendency often takes the specific form of the demography-as-destiny argument. In light of predictions that we will soon become a country with no racial majority, the widespread belief, among racial progressives and conservatives alike, is that once achieved this magical tipping point will be of practical as well as symbolic importance.

Color me skeptical on two fronts. The racial-tipping-point argument assumes we will have similar racial identity options then as now, that the meanings of racial categories will be similar, and/or that similarly situated people will make similar identity choices then as they do now. All this is doubtful. However, even if or when the no-majority shift comes, is it necessarily the case that numbers equal power? Not for blacks in South Africa, or Shi'as in Iraq, or peasants in China, or women around the world. For that matter, do people of color and poor and working-class whites in the United States have social, political, or economic clout remotely in proportion to their numbers now?

Envisioning the desirable racial future we want is hugely important if we are to craft the strategies and muster the support we need to work effectively toward it. It is also difficult, ambitious work. Most of us are hard-pressed to imagine a future substantially different than our present, especially a truly transformative one brought about mainly by thoughtful strategies and action rather than magical thinking. To these creative challenges I highlight one more, arguably the most formidable of all: seeing beyond the race-as-problem narrative.

Race in the United States is widely regarded as a monstrously ugly and intractable problem. The *New York Times* recently reported a national survey finding that less than one-third of black Americans and one-half of white Americans say we have made "a lot" of progress on race. The biggest U.S. race stories of 2013 featured the killing of an unarmed black teenager by a "half-Latino, half-White" neighborhood watch coordinator and the latter's subsequent acquittal by an all-white jury; the admission by a white celebrity chef that she has used the "N-word"; and the Supreme Court's scuttling of the Voting Rights Act.

Many Americans believe we have been overzealous in our efforts to right the racial wrongs of the past. Perceptions of "reverse racism" against whites and cynical manipulation of the "race card" by people of color means that talk about race will often meet with resentment and hostility rather than interest or sympathy. Even from the perspective of social and racial justice advocates, race is a problem. We have very different ideas than many others do about what the problem is, exactly, and how to deal with it, but the race-as-problem frame is central to our narratives as well. Much of this essay is a case in point.

We need to recognize the story of race in America as a more expansive one than its public, largely media-wrought portrait suggests. What the novelist and social critic James Baldwin once said of himself could be said of race itself: "I am what time, circumstance, history, have made of me, certainly, but I am also much more than that."

Think about the meaning that so many found in Barack Obama's presidential campaign and victory in 2008. To be sure, the seventy million Obama voters brought a range of motives to their polling stations. For many, the viability of Obama's candidacy and his eventual triumph marked a crucial milestone in the centuries-long struggle for racial justice and inclusion in the United States. For others, the election was (also) a referendum on the Bush years, the merits of the McCain/Palin ticket, and/or something else entirely. However, running powerfully through all of it was something else I had felt strongly in the wake of the 9/11 attacks, and in the countless acts of compassion that buoyed the Gulf Coast after Hurricanes Katrina and Rita.

This something, I believe, was a yearning for human connectedness whose realization so often founders on the shoals of race and the fears and resentments associated with it. Obama's biography and vision invited us to believe that we could repair our disconnectedness. In no other country on earth, he said, was his story even possible. Here was the update on Ronald Reagan's "shining city on a hill," retold through the lens of a black man's personal story. Obama invoked the better angels of our national character and said we could choose to have them define us. That, in my view, was the core promise of his "politics of hope." Rather than being a problem, race was the main vehicle for that inspiring work.

We see echoes of this, as well, in National Public Radio's Race Card Project. NPR's Michele Norris asked people to "think about their experiences, questions, hopes, dreams, laments or observations about race and identity" and to distill those thoughts into six or fewer words on a postcard. A visit to the Race Card Project's online wall confirms that, for some respondents, race is indeed something other than, and certainly much more than, a terrible problem. Here is a sample of the postcards submitted.

> Vietnamese is Difficult. Love is stronger.
> Adobo Beef Stew Rice Potatoes: Dinner.
> In Eugene, I miss the colors.
> Uncovering lost migration stories, increasing empathy.
> I see myself in the other.
> Understanding began with racially mixed family.

We miss each other so much.
Hearts changed. Adopted from Ethiopia. FAMILY.

Here we see race construed as bridgeable distance, as community, as a vehicle for personal and social transformation and connection. If we are to envision a world and country in which race still matters, but is seen much less as an ugly, intractable problem and much more as a social salve, we could do worse than to build on these insights.

CONCLUSION

Like radon gas, hidden racial bias is odorless, colorless, and its presence is easily disguised. Left untreated, both are dangerous, even deadly. For those of us who espouse racially egalitarian ideals, removing our hidden biases from the cognitive shadows that nurture them is a necessary step toward more consistently walking our values talk. However, if we are to create a society in which our culture no longer provides the seedbed for pervasive unconscious bias, we must choose to walk that path. This is aspirational work. We have a lot of talking, and walking, to do.

Chapter Seven

A Personal Reflection—The Battle for Diversity on Campus

The Supreme Court, Civil Rights Research, and Affirmative Action in the Twenty-First Century

Gary Orfield

Affirmative action in college admissions is about a half century old and it has always been contentious, with the public divided and a divided Supreme Court accepting it only with a narrow rationale and with increasing skepticism. But, before we look at the legal struggle, where critics suggest that there is a great conflict, I would like to start with personal experience. I've been listening to all the discussion about how hard diversity is, but as I write, I'm thinking about an undergraduate class I taught recently. There were 150 undergraduate students in it, extremely diverse, dealing with many of the rights issues that divide the country. And I'm just thinking about my morning office hours, when I talked to one student after another student—Latino, African American, Korean American, white—students from very different economic backgrounds and communities. All of these students experienced the extremely intense interchanges that happened in class about issues of educational equity, and they gained new understandings of their own situations, of how they got there, of what their society is about. Of course their conclusions were not all the same, but they all showed some serious reflection and awareness of other perspectives, strongly expressed, that often challenged their own. And they were engaged and interested, and it was very, very fascinating to teach them and to listen to them thinking hard.

Always when we're thinking about the difficulty of achieving diversity, we should be thinking about the amazing things that happen when you really do cross these lines, and you really do understand each other, and you really do reflect on your society and understand it in new ways. Many of these students were thinking about their lives and possible careers in new ways. It was a pretty thrilling kind of educational experience to teach these students in this setting and see them learning from each other, clarifying and sometimes changing their own understanding and their own values. I think that's what

72

we should be trying to do on diverse campuses. Often it happens without our effort, just in discussions in coffee shops or dorm rooms. It's difficult sometimes, but really difficult in a very healthy, stimulating, exciting way. We need to always look at students and realize that they will be living in a vastly more diverse society even than what we know today and that it may either turn out something like the class or be afflicted with even deeper divisions, stereotypes, and inequality. What happens in the colleges that train our leaders and form our professions matters.

So, we are a multiracial country with unequal access to higher education, which is essential for success. We're falling behind many other nations in college graduation levels. For many years we were the first in the world. We're now about sixteenth. And a lot of that is because we're simply not graduating the students of color in our society. We have been resegregating our public schools now ever since the early 1990s, under decisions of the Rehnquist Court, and we're now back to levels of segregation from the middle 1960s. Resegregation is especially severe for black students in the South and for Latino students in the West, who are extremely isolated at schools with, on average, twice as many poor kids as white students have contact with. And these schools are disadvantaged in terms of course offerings, teacher qualifications, level of competition, graduation rates, and many other things.

In our higher education system, we have two roots of the segregation of higher education. First, nineteen states until the civil rights era maintained separate colleges and universities for black students. They were segregated by law. And those states have always been home to most black students in the United States; they still are today. Texas is one of those states. Those states were, of course, legally obligated to take steps to disestablish their dual systems of higher education. Standards were set in the Carter administration, but they were never followed. They were interpreted away by the Reagan administration. There's been very little pressure on those states' colleges since that time.

The other affirmative action in higher education really came from the tradition of the elite colleges in the North and the West. These colleges had virtually no minority students until the 1960s, when they adopted voluntary desegregation efforts in response to the civil rights movement, their feeling that they needed to, and from some pressure by the federal government.

The most favorable conditions for diversity came when college spaces were rapidly expanding, tuition was low, financial aid was ample, and the courts weren't limiting what universities could do. And in the late 1970s, we actually achieved the most equal access to higher education we've experienced to date. The Supreme Court's *Bakke* decision was a limited success, preserving affirmative action, but also limiting it. Shortly after that, we began to raise college costs every year, faster than family incomes. We cut the Pell Grants in the Reagan era of the 1980s. We did a lot of things that made college less accessible, and those things continued as the states went through tremendous financial cutbacks of the Great Recession.

Affirmative action went on for a generation before its first test in the Supreme Court, in the 1978 *Bakke* case, a quarter century before the next in the 2003 *Grutter* decision, but less than a decade before the third test in the 2012 *Fisher* case and only two years before the 2014 *Schuette* decision. In *Bakke*, affirmative action was saved by a single vote but at the price of narrowing its justification. The Court said that it could not be defended as compensating for a history of inequality and discrimination but only because universities had the right to pursue educationally beneficial diversity; race could not be considered on its own, but only as a "plus factor" in a complex admissions process. In *Grutter* and the companion *Gratz* the Michigan undergraduate method of adding plus points for various forms of diversity including race was rejected as too mechanical, but the law school's more searching "holistic" review was accepted. In the *Fisher* case we were at risk of losing the right that almost all of our selective institutions want to have to select their students in a way that produces a diverse student body because the Supreme Court had become more conservative with the replacement of Justice Sandra Day O'Connor by Justice Samuel Alito. It had become the most conservative Supreme Court in generations as shown in its dramatic curtailment of voluntary school integration. In *Schuette* the Court upheld the racially tinged referenda that have written prohibitions on affirmative action into state constitutions.

The Civil Rights Project and associated scholars from many universities have carried out a continuing program of research on college opportunity and worked very actively on briefs in *Grutter*, *Fisher*, and *Schuette*. A radical court could have actually taken away from colleges their right to admit diverse classes, superimposing the judgment of a court on the autonomy of all of our educational institutions, and making decisions of tremendous consequence for the future of our society, since our society is a very stratified society and leadership positions are very linked to access to selective higher education. The *Fisher* ruling has delayed the possibility of that, for now by sending it back to the lower courts for more information, but schools are still at risk of losing their autonomy. Rather than deferring to a university's own determination that race-neutral means are insufficient to obtain the benefits of a diverse student body, the *Fisher* decision emphasized that admissions plans must be closely examined and that the final determination of whether any consideration of race is legal remains strictly in the hands of the federal court judges.

We're in a time when one would think we would be working from the other side of the diversity puzzle—thinking about what more needs to be done in addition to affirmative action. Affirmative action has not been that great. With affirmative action still operating in all fifty states, black students still have one-fifth the chance of white students to attend a selective university. Latino students have one-third the chance. And it's been declining in the last twenty years. That is because it's becoming more competitive to get into these institutions, there's more demand for them, spaces have not been adequately expanded, and as the racial proportions of the society change, the relative access to these institutions for nonwhite students has been declining.

We're in a great racial transition. Nearly half of the students in our public schools are nonwhite. If you look at the first-grade population in fall 2009 it was 49 percent nonwhite. If you look at the population of the South or the West, they're already predominately nonwhite. In the West only about two-fifths of the students are white and there are already more Latinos than whites. Very soon, whites are going to be one of a number of minority groups in the society, and it's pretty obvious that we all have to get along or it won't work well.

If you were to come to my part of the country in Southern California, 75 percent of the students in the public schools already are not white. We have to figure out how to educate the students we actually have, and the growing numbers are mostly among Latinos, who have the worst success in higher education. That's why businesses, the universities, the military, and the other institutions that have a long-term perspective on the society are thinking about this issue. They don't have the luxury of just thinking about the next election campaign or the next soundbite. They have to think about who is going to actually be there and how we can get them ready to do the jobs and lead our institutions. The population of high school graduates is declining, both the birthrate and net migration have declined sharply, and we have to work with the students we have to succeed as a society.

Though we don't have the population that we had in the past, we have institutions, practices and beliefs that are designed around that white middle-class population. Those students are and will continue to be a declining share of the demographic of this nation. We have to change our institutions and our practices if it's all going to work. Civil rights has a critical role to play.

We thought before *Fisher* that the affirmative action issue was settled for at least a generation or so after the huge effort the University of Michigan and its supporters made in the *Grutter* case and *Gratz* case in 2003. Justice O'Connor's majority opinion in *Grutter* talked of twenty-five years. But it was opened again all of a sudden. The issue came in a very strange and inappropriate case. *Fisher* was not a class action case. It's a case of one student, Abigail Fisher, who wanted to go to the University of Texas. The University of Texas said she wouldn't have been admitted even if there had been no affirmative action, because she wasn't qualified. Also, she didn't really want to go. She had already graduated from Louisiana State University. Her name is just on that case because a well-financed conservative group in Washington wanted to find a way to bring this case and bring it from the University of Texas, because they have a very well-publicized alternative admissions process called the "Percent Plan" that has been said to be an adequate substitute. Because most alternative plans have been obvious failures, this could be their strongest case to challenge the necessity of affirmative action.

This case was taken by the Supreme Court in spite of all kinds of procedural flaws and difficulties. So the Supreme Court wanted it—at least the four justices whose votes were needed to put it on the docket—and they wanted to take it, presumably, because it could be used to attack affirmative action. This is a very activist court. It's the court that has really created a plutocracy in the United States through the *Citizens United* case and slashed voting rights. It's the court that radically reinterpreted the Second Amendment to prohibit locally enacted limits on guns. It's the court that, of course, in the public school desegregation case from Seattle and Louisville, discarded decades of precedents in favor of voluntary action by school districts to produce school integration and created radical limits on the capacity of school districts to do things, even voluntarily through choice systems. It's a court that, when it takes a case, civil rights lawyers tremble. In the Warren Court era, people thought justice was going to be expanded when the Court took a case. In this Court, civil rights lawyers expect it will be contracted.

This is a very closely divided Court. There is a one-vote majority for a lot of its most important decisions. So our Constitution hangs on one vote. In the 2003 Michigan affirmative action case, it hung on the vote of Sandra Day O'Connor. Sandra Day O'Connor, although she was conservative herself, was replaced by the much more conservative Justice Samuel Alito. Civil rights experts feared that would lead to a limit or prohibition on affirmative action in universities. The relatively recent precedent, *Grutter*, was being challenged in an obviously inappropriate case.

The Supreme Court usually takes a case when there is division among the lower courts. There was no division before *Fisher*. It usually takes a case with a record that has been well developed. This case was not well developed. The University of Texas simply said that they were obeying the law: "We're doing what the Michigan case said." There wasn't a rich development of facts. So one of the problems that we had in the research community was in questioning how well the Supreme Court could make a decision about the future of diversity in higher education with highly imperfect information that came out of the briefs from the parties in the case about one student. The University of Texas did not do the job that the University of Michigan did in spending millions and creating a big body of research and information, nor did it do the job in mobilizing briefs and support for explaining a case to the country, so it was a very difficult set of circumstances.

The *Fisher* Court eventually upheld the value of diversity in promoting important educational benefits, in addressing racial isolation and stereotypes, and in preparing students for leadership in a diverse society, consistent with the Court's previous rulings in *Bakke* and *Grutter v. Bollinger*. The decision shifted the focus from proving the benefits of diversity, which the court conceded, to the more complex questions of whether university admissions policies were narrowly tailored with no more consideration of race beyond what was necessary to advance the compelling interest in diversity. If there was a workable nonracial alternative, race could not be considered. Rather than deferring to a university's own determination that race-neutral means are insufficient to obtain the benefits of a diverse student body, the *Fisher* Court emphasized that admissions plans must be closely examined and that the final determination of constitutionality remains in the hands of the courts. The Court held that the lower courts misinterpreted the *Grutter* standards by allowing greater deference to the University of Texas in showing that the institution had explored workable race-neutral alternatives before adopting a race-conscious policy. The Supreme Court remanded the case back to the lower courts to evaluate the evidence under a more stringent standard. So now universities have to convince judges that they have tried feasible alternatives and they did not produce sufficient diversity to create the desired educational benefits.

The *Grutter* decision was a great victory following a huge mobilization around the country. The Civil Rights Project was created at Harvard in 1996 in part because of the abolition that year of affirmative action in California and Texas. When we learned then that there was almost no research going on about the critical issues coming before the court we decided to create a research center that would generate a new body of research about these and other civil rights issues. There was research commissioned and some of it came into play in the *Grutter* decision and was cited by the court. We felt that we were at least on a path to maintain affirmative action, which is a limited but very important tool.

Every Supreme Court case is a combination of findings of fact and findings of the law. Where do the facts come from? They usually—in a normal case—come from the briefs of the parties and the record of the trial. But in these cases which have huge national implications, people have been adding to that discussion by increasing the information that gets submitted to the court and comes from a variety of sources through amicus briefs, often aimed at the Justices thought to have the most potential influence on the outcome. Justice Kennedy, who people knew was the only possible vote that might be changed in *Fisher*, had voted against affirmative action in the *Grutter* case, interpreting the Michigan Law School procedure not as a model for diversity, but as an implicit hidden quota. His history created great challenges. So it was very important to address his issues.

The *Parents Involved* decision, the public school case that was decided in 2007, created some really serious problems for civil rights and it helped lead to the *Fisher* case. Basically, the lower courts had all said voluntary school integration was fine, it was good. It had been encouraged by courts for years.

The Bush administration and conservatives challenged and the Supreme Court limited, in Justice Kennedy's controlling opinion, the use by school districts of choice plans that consciously were aimed at creating integration. It undermined those very seriously. So this set the stage for the challenge that came along in *Fisher*. Kennedy said, in the *Parents Involved* case, that diversity, school integration, is a compelling interest for the country. But he then took away most of the means of doing it.

From a civil rights standpoint, the best thing that could have happened in the *Fisher* case—had it reached a decision on the basic issues—was a tie vote, since Justice Kagan had recused herself because she was involved in this case in the early stage in the Justice Department before joining the Court. What we got instead was a large majority sending the key question back to the lower courts, which must grapple with the issues we researched in the *Fisher* briefs.

Texas has a very widely publicized alternative, the Percent Plan, which affirmative action opponents claim actually produces adequate diversity. So the challenge we faced when we started thinking about this case was: what can be done to strengthen the record after a trial that produced limited evidence? We knew there were two big issues that would be raised in the case. One would be the "compelling interest," whether or not the evidence is compelling about the educational value of diversity.

We didn't think that was going to be a central issue because Justice Kennedy had said before that he believes diversity is a compelling interest. But, in any case, it was necessary to update that research and to put it before the Court. The American Education Research Association, together with the American Statistical Association and many national associations, filed briefs doing that, and doing it quite effectively, summarizing the research, particularly work produced in the last nine years since the last Supreme Court decision on affirmative action. It turned out that the compelling interest issue did not divide the Court, at least in this case. The value of diverse educational experiences was simply accepted.

Some of the issues that we wanted to raise simply can't be raised in the Supreme Court these days, because the *Bakke* decision itself said societal discrimination is irrelevant as a justification for affirmative action. That conclusion erases great chunks of history. If you look at Texas, the public schools are and always have been very segregated. They're very unequal—as they are in almost all of our states—there is severe societal discrimination that has always existed.

The effects of a long history of slavery, apartheid, and segregation of both blacks and Latinos and the conquest and dispossession of Mexican and American Indian groups have never been overcome to the extent that there is anything like equal opportunity for young people. But we can't talk about the high schools in this case, because that would be considered societal discrimination, though the impact on ability to meet college entrance standards without affirmative action is obvious, so we have to talk about other issues that are still on the table after the judicial limitations that were basic in both the *Bakke* case and the *Grutter* case. The Court doesn't want to think about the whole system of educational inequality that exists in the country though it is all connected.

The Supreme Court majority in this and other areas of civil rights has simply been adopting a view that serious discrimination has vanished and that there are no continuing effects of the history of blatant discrimination that need to be considered. The court became very conservative during the twenty-five-year period in which no justices were appointed by Democratic presidents, and the court created many precedents limiting civil rights during this period.

There has been a majority of civil rights conservatives on the Court that took hold by the late 1980s and early 1990s and persists to today. That's what we're dealing with, so we can't talk in briefs about a lot of things that seem very logically connected to social science research. What we decided to do when we were thinking about this case was to try to give some voice to the researchers around the country that have been working on this issue for decades. Researchers have a lot of information that is relevant. In the brief that we organized, which was ultimately signed by 444 scholars from forty-two states, we tried to talk about whether there really is an alternative to affirmative action since you can't consider race in admissions if it's not really essential for achieving diversity.

So we decided to give the Court the best research findings we could identify on that key issue. We created a network of researchers around the country, basically an electronic network that would "meet" every Friday on a conference call to try to think about what was known about these issues, and what we could fit into the context of a Supreme Court brief. A number of researchers drafted sections of the brief. You only get nine thousand words—maximum—and that's thirty-six pages to deal with all the complicated issues that you're trying to explain to the Court. And of course, you have to put in a lot of legal framing for the social science discussion.

We hired a young postdoc, Liliana Garces, who had worked with the Civil Rights Project both at Harvard and UCLA and was at the University of Michigan during that time. She became our counsel of record. She has a doctorate in education from Harvard and is a wonderful young scholar now teaching at Pennsylvania State University. We had experts who wrote memos every week and collected data and research from everywhere. We found that there were many people who wanted to participate in this. They all volunteered. Nobody got paid anything for doing that work and a lot of the logistics were coordinated by a brilliant young undergraduate at UCLA. We put together draft after draft of a brief.

Our idea wasn't to "cook up" a brief that was going to be the typical partisan brief. It was to try to create a brief that actually reflected a broad consensus in the social science world—in other words trying to tell the truth to power. And the truth is complicated, of course. One of the problems of many civil rights lawsuits—I've been involved in dozens of them—is that both sides produce a set of arguments that are so one-sided that they are not very convincing, and the judge throws up his hands and says there's a war of the experts, so we'll just decide on whatever our basic assumption or prejudices are about these things.

We tried to raise a number of issues. One of them was the link between the Percent Plan and segregation. The Percent Plan in Texas says anybody in the top 10 percent of his or her graduating class in more than one thousand high schools all over Texas has an absolute right to go to the University of Texas at Austin. It only produces some diversity because of the intense segregation of schools in Texas, so it is not race conscious at the individual level but is race conscious at the school level, exploiting the fact that since the schools are segregated in Texas, the many segregated Latino schools and the much smaller group of segregated black schools automatically produce top 10 percenters who are nonwhite. But what we found out is that those schools will produce top 10 percenters who are Latino, since there are many more Latinos and they are more segregated than blacks in Texas now, but rarely will they produce black students.

There are very few segregated black schools left in Texas. Even though an eighth of Texas' students are black, they tend to be in schools, on average, that have only one-third blacks in them, and they have often more Latinos than blacks. So they're segregated from whites, they're segregated from the middle class, they are segregated from many pre-collegiate opportunities, but they're not segregated in all-Black schools. The Percent Plan just doesn't work very well for blacks or the state's small American Indian population.

The *Fisher* brief claimed that the Percent Plan had produced a wonderful recovery of diversity so we don't have to worry about affirmative action. But they lumped the Blacks and Latinos together as if they were all interchangeable—anybody who is nonwhite—even though Texas has an incredible history of overt discrimination against blacks in de jure segregation throughout most of its history. The brief for *Fisher* didn't note several key facts in the claim that the Percent Plan had solved the problem: (1) that the number of Latino students in the state's schools actually had doubled since affirmative action was first ended in 1996, so getting back to the same number actually reflected a much lower probability of a Latino student's access, (2) the share of whites has plummeted among the high school population of Texas, so if you come back to the proportions you had back in 1996, you're not succeeding. Students of color actually had a much lower level of access to the university than they had before.

We worked to figure out how to explain to the judges some of these issues. Judges aren't trained in statistics. So how do you take statistical information and explain it to people who don't understand statistics? We also tried to show that if this case became a way to decide the issue for the whole country, there were going to be a lot of places where the plan simply would not be applicable. Ninety percent of the students in Texas go to universities in Texas. In many states, lots of students go to universities out of state, so the Percent Plan wouldn't work there. Private universities do not define their universe as one state, so the top 10 percent in one state won't work there. For example, most of the students in Massachusetts go to private universities. It wouldn't work there. How could it work for transfer students, since it is based on high school class position? It wouldn't work, but transfer students are a very important source of students in upper divisions of many public universities. How could it work for graduate and professional schools? It wouldn't.

You don't choose graduate and professional students from ranking students in their high school graduating class in one state. So one of the things we were trying to explain in our few words was that there would be very large and important sectors of education and many institutions that would not be able to use this, even if they decided it had worked well enough in Texas. Secondly, we underlined that it really didn't provide a level of access equivalent to what had existed previously.

We produced a lot of information from California, which has been without affirmative action since 1996. The percentage of Chicano and Latino applicants who were admitted to the University of California in 1995 from those who applied and who were qualified (because you can only get into the University of California system if you're in the top eighth of the high school population) was 50 percent. It's now 12.9 percent, one-fourth of the chance of getting admitted compared to what existed before. If you were Latino and you applied in 1995, your chance of getting admitted to UC Berkeley was 61 percent, compared to 13.9 percent in 2010. For African American students back in 1995, if you applied and you were fully qualified for the University of California, your chances of getting admitted to Berkeley were 50 percent; in 2010 it was 12.9 percent. So we've had a tremendous loss of potential diversity. We almost lost black student representation altogether in the under-graduate college at UCLA several years ago. We had only ninety-five black students admitted to our entire freshman class.

At the most selective University of California campuses now, you have to have an A-plus average to get in. And you usually get the A-plus average by being in a high school that has a lot of AP courses and advanced work, which are counted more highly, and, of course, those classes are distributed very unequally in the California public schools, which are extremely segregated. Even more than in Texas, the African American students are locked into Latino schools of highly concentrated poverty now. There are very few all African American schools left in California. We actually tried a percent plan at the University of California and it didn't work. It had almost no impact, and we have tried a lot of other things such as outreach programs. But one of the real problems is that over time these things get defunded, and if demand grows much more rapidly than spaces for students, the competition becomes extremely intense. The university's outreach and support programs didn't work very well, but they were better than nothing, and now they've been substantially defunded.

So we tried to explain a lot of issues in our brief. Rather than stigma being caused by affirmative action, a favorite topic of Justice Clarence Thomas, for example, new research shows students feel more color positive where there is affirmative action. In the University of California system, the African American and Latino students who are admitted to our most elite campuses don't feel better because there's no affirmative action. They actually feel much more isolated and less comfortable on the campuses. The theory of stigma would suggest that since none of them have been admitted through affirmative action or any race-conscious policy, they should feel free of this stigma that conservatives think is caused by affirmative action. We also found that the most talented African American and Latino students, whom the University of California wants the most, are not even coming to our elite campuses anymore. They're going someplace else, because they don't feel welcome and part of a really diverse community on our campuses. So contrary to the stigma theory, the minority students at the University of Texas, where there still is affirmative action, actually feel more accepted and more welcome and more desirous of coming to the campus than at the University of California.

We created a brief and distributed it to hundreds of experts for review and possible signatures. We got suggestions for changes in this regular scholarly process. The drafting committee was like the ultimate peer review every week. We strengthened and modified the document and had much more material than would fit within the Court's page limit. We then had student volunteers go check to make sure that everybody who signed it really was working at their university or their research center, because we didn't want anyone who really wasn't qualified to sign it. We even received requests from people in other countries trying to sign it. The brief was ultimately signed by 444 scholars, from 172 U.S. universities and research centers, and we presented the findings at the National Press Club in Washington before the argument of the case.

There was almost no coverage of this presentation. The newspapers were much more interested in covering a brief by one professor at UCLA, Richard Sander, who was making a career out of arguing that African American students and Latino students who get admitted to law school under affirmative action don't do as well on the bar exam; therefore, they should go to less elite schools. There have been many refutations, including studies by Richard Lempert of the University of Michigan and William Kidder of UC Riverside, but the press has not covered this debate very well. And the university hasn't done very much in terms of public relations and public affairs. Often, in our experience, academic attacks on civil rights are treated as important news while studies showing benefits receive little attention.

Now, if you're thinking about how research is related to the possible meaning of the broad terms in the Constitution, you have to realize that the Court doesn't have to look at any of this material. Even though the vast majority of research that we identified shows that affirmative action has positive advantages and that there really are not good alternatives, in the earlier school desegregation case dealing with some similar issues, the chief justice dismissed the research signed by most of the country's leading scholars in the field as nothing more than part of a war of the experts that could simply be ignored in that decision. He felt no need to pay attention to any of the research reflecting the broad consensus. There is also a network of conservative think tanks that generate conflicting briefs and societies, such as the Federalist Society, that foster conservative causes and are closely linked to several members of the Supreme Court.

We thought it was very important that there be a voice from the research community, both in the AERA brief and in the Brief of American Social Scientists that we worked on with scholars around the country, because we think it's important that the truth—as best we can judge it—be out there, and challenge a history of backward movement on educational rights.

We didn't know what was going to happen, but we knew that it was important to have this voice for scholars in this case, trying to put good information before the Court and the country. We were greatly surprised by the 7–1 decision that left the basic law of affirmative action in place for the time being but raised the stakes for colleges convincing judges that there was no alternative way to achieve diversity.

After the Supreme Court decision, the court of appeals reviewed the *Fisher* case and the majority documented at length in its 2014 decision the ways in which the University of Texas had tried alternatives and had found none to be workable. But a strong dissenting opinion held that the university had failed to specify and justify how much diversity (the critical mass) was needed for its educational diversity and held that its plan should not be acceptable. Probable demands for rehearing by the full court of appeals or reconsideration by the Supreme Court guarantee that the issues will continue both in Texas and across the country.

Our research did not turn out to play any visible role in the *Fisher* non-decision, but it may well be used as the issue continues to evolve. We are now working with the Educational Testing Service in commissioning and reviewing a series of studies on the issues still pending after *Fisher* and with the American Council on Education and other organizations in finding out how colleges have or have not altered their admissions procedures following *Fisher* and what help they may need.

We need to have a long perspective. We need to train young people to participate in these efforts. And we need to think about the Court. This is a one-vote majority Court. This Court could be changed by an appointment perhaps after the 2016 presidential election. And then we would be in a different constitutional world, and the data and the research that was done, which might be ignored now, could come back to life then. If a conservative Court can throw away a precedent that's deeply rooted, another Court can change it back, exactly what Abraham Lincoln said in the aftermath of the Dred Scott decision, which reinforced slavery. He said that if there's a narrowly divided Court that defies precedent and that makes an unjust decision on poor evidence, it's the job of people to continuously try to change it. There was a very intense, very political effort to change the Warren Court from something that was supportive of rights for students of color to one that is hostile to minority rights. There has to be a similar effort to change it back, so it becomes a Court that can speak for a country with the kind of diversity that we're going to have.

Our brief, the work that supports it, the work of the American Education Research Association and others who participated in *Fisher* are on the web. They should be distributed as widely as possible. They're worth reading. And of course the transcript of the Supreme Court's oral argument, the recording of it, is also on the web. It's a sobering experience to read and listen to those discussions. Scholars and those who wish to participate in the national debates over the future of racial justice in America should keep informed.

Our work is part of generations of struggle to broaden opportunity, and it is not a smooth or easy path. Most efforts show no immediate impact or are ignored or even rejected in the decisions. Sometimes there is a great success. Those of us in the research community must share in the long battle to give real educational opportunity to groups of students who have never truly experienced it. Research and knowledge are not, in themselves, sufficient to accomplish change, but they can help direct efforts, inform discussion, and improve the quality of policy when good policies are adopted. When there are losses and policy turns in ways that will do still more harm to equal opportunity, those of us who do this work must do it again and again and again, working to make it more powerful and more intelligible and to insert it as well as we can into the policy and legal debates until justice has been achieved.

Chapter Eight

School Integration in the Post–*Parents Involved* Era

Erica Frankenburg

The country, and public school enrollment, is more racially diverse than ever before. Yet, at a time when public schools enroll more black and Latino students, we also see deepening segregation for these students on a wider geographic scale and when we are learning more about the costs to students and society of racial segregation. Patterns of increasing segregation are particularly strong in the regions of the country that are the most diverse (and populous): Latinos are severely segregated from whites in the West while black students are resegregating at a rapid rate in the South (Orfield, Kucsera, and Siegel-Hawley 2012). Schools with concentrations of black and/or Latino students are usually also schools of concentrated poverty.

These trends are troubling because of the increasing knowledge about the costs of segregation and the benefits of integration. Nearly sixty years ago, the U.S. Supreme Court in *Brown v. Board of Education* declared that racially segregated schools were inherently unequal and research continues to support this seminal judicial determination. In particular, there is a growing body of literature that finds long-term effects on students' life opportunities if they attend segregated schools. Segregated students are likely to have lower post-graduation earnings and lower educational attainment, and are more likely to be incarcerated than their peers who attend more integrated settings. Further, students of all races benefit from diverse schools in ways that are important for our communities: they are more likely to live and work in diverse communities as adults, for example.

In 2007, the U.S. Supreme Court decided a case, *Parents Involved in Community Schools v. Seattle School District No. 1*, involving the voluntary integration policies of two school districts (Seattle, Washington, and Jefferson County, Kentucky, which includes Louisville and surrounding suburbs). In a long, fractured decision, the Court made several important holdings.

First, relying in part on some of the research described above about the harms of racial isolation and benefits of diverse schools, a majority of the Court endorsed two compelling interests, or the constitutionality of integration policy goals, focusing on (1) reducing racial isolation in schools and (2) increasing school diversity. (The Court had similarly found in *Grutter v. Bollinger* in 2003 that these goals were important aims for colleges and universities.) Second, a majority of the justices also held that the districts' policies as designed were unconstitutional because they weren't "narrowly tailored" to achieve the districts' goals. In other words, the Court believed that making student assignment decisions that took into account an individual student's race unfairly stigmatized that student, and this injury violated the Fourteenth Amendment. Justice Kennedy's decision also invoked several possible ways districts could continue to pursue integration that would be considered constitutional.

Parents Involved was the latest of a string of school desegregation decisions by the Supreme Court beginning with *Milliken v. Bradley* in 1974 and persisting through three decisions in the 1990s that limited first the extent to which desegregation was required by school districts that had mandated racially separate schools and subsequently, in *Parents Involved*, limited the policies districts had voluntarily adopted to integrate students. Ironically, where the Court in the 1954 *Brown* decision ruled that districts' use of race to assign students to segregated schools was unconstitutional, they now found that using students' race to assign students to integrated schools was unconstitutional. In just over fifty years, the Court's understanding of race and education had shifted markedly, leading Justice Stevens to write a dissent lamenting the Court's decision and how far he'd seen their jurisprudence shift since he had joined the Court decades earlier.

At a time of increasing restrictions on what districts can do in terms of designing policy to break the historically strong link between school and neighborhood segregation, demographic analysis finds slight decreases in residential segregation but, in many metropolitan areas, neighborhoods remain segregated. What is of particular concern is that the link between residential and school segregation has strengthened during the last decade (Frankenberg 2013b), which suggests that an additional strategy to pursue for school desegregation advocates should be efforts to further housing integration. Indeed, had residential segregation not declined, it is likely that school segregation increases would have been larger (see also Reardon and Yun 2005).

With these legal and demographic trends in mind, the remainder of this chapter turns to analyzing the response to K–12 school segregation generally and the *Parents Involved* decision in particular. I review, in turn, the response from the federal government, federal courts, and local governments (e.g., school districts). I describe the varied patterns of response from these different actors with regard to school integration efforts after *Parents Involved*.

FEDERAL GOVERNMENT

When *Parents Involved* was decided, George W. Bush was president, and his administration had proven to be quite hostile to advancing civil rights (see Le 2010). The politicization of the Justice Department and Bush appointees to the U.S. Civil Rights Commission, combined with the Department of Education's reversal on key civil rights positions adopted under the Clinton administration, together resulted in an atmosphere in which even information about the extent of desegregation was challenged, much less were activities to further integration undertaken. For example, the Bush administration had filed briefs in the *Parents Involved* case urging the Court to strike down the districts' policies, which was a reversal of its position in similar lower court cases. It also tried to end many long-running desegregation cases to which the Department of Justice was a party (Le, 2010). The latter is a concern because of trends finding an increase in segregation after court-ordered desegregation has ended. Finally, it released a series of "Dear Colleague" letters about what was permissible in student assignment and school choice that were hostile to any use of race and even skeptical of the goals of diversity in K–12 education.

Racial justice advocates had high hopes for the Obama administration that took office in 2009, although action proved to be slower in coming than originally hoped. One of the requests by advocates was to revoke the 2008 "Dear Colleague" letter issued by the Bush Department of Education about the *Parents Involved* decision. It wasn't until December 2011 that the Departments of Education and Justice jointly released comprehensive guidance about permissible means to pursue K–12 voluntary integration replacing the 2008 letter. The guidance strongly affirmed the importance of diversity in elementary and secondary schools, citing cases from *Brown* to *Parents Involved* to buttress their recognition of compelling interests in reducing racial isolation and promoting diversity. After explaining how the departments interpreted the legal framework in *Parents Involved*, the guidance provided lengthy discussions of how to practically apply the legal framework to schools. The guidance, for instance, specified both race-conscious and race-neutral approaches that would be constitutional and listed a comprehensive set of steps that districts should consider in implementing such programs. Finally, it concluded with concrete examples of illustrative approaches that districts could consider to create diverse schools or reduce racial isolation. Though delayed, the comprehensive nature of the guidance may be particularly useful in making sense of the complicated *Parents Involved* decision for local district officials.

Another promising program to offer school districts technical assistance to revise their student assignment plans was announced by the Obama administration but congressional authorization for this funding began during the Bush administration. This small grant program, Technical Assistance for Student Assignment Plans (TASAP), offered eleven districts up to $250,000 that was competitively awarded based on their proposed activities and need. Research on this program has found mixed results: in a number of districts, school boards adopted new assignment policies or made improvements to the implementation of existing student assignment policies (DeBray, McDermott, Frankenberg, and Blankenship 2012). In a few districts, local politics changed districts' proposed plans, and these districts adopted policies that are likely to exacerbate segregation (Frankenberg, McDermott, DeBray, and Blankenship, 2012). Since many of the changes are relatively recent, further research is needed to fully understand the impact of TASAP.

In addition to TASAP, the other major federal funding source that can help districts pursue integration is the Magnet School Assistance Program (MSAP), although in recent years it had become less effective in reducing racial isolation because the Bush Department of Education required magnet schools to use race-neutral criteria for admissions. A subsequent evaluation of magnet school grant recipients found that requiring race neutrality has harmed grant recipients' effectiveness at reducing or eliminating racial isolation. In 2010, the first MSAP funding cycle under the Obama administration, the criteria were tightened to focus on fewer goals, one of them being reducing racial isolation. The department also changed the definition of racial isolation to comply with *Parents Involved*, to more flexibly consider definitions of diversity that go beyond a white-nonwhite binary. The most recent MSAP cycle in 2013 extends the 2010 guidelines as they relate to racial isolation and diversity and refers applicants to the 2011 guidance. Significantly, applicants are required to show proof of adoption of a voluntary desegregation plan or court-ordered desegregation plan as part of their application.

Finally, by virtue of not being the Bush administration's Office of Civil Rights (in the Department of Education) and Justice Department, these departments under the Obama administration have already been more favorable to K–12 integration because they have ended efforts that were hostile to desegregation. The Office of Civil Rights (OCR) has a wide range of responsibilities for K–12 education including providing technical assistance (in accordance with the guidance listed above), certifying the MSAP grantees have acceptable desegregation plans, and investigating complaints. In the OCR's publication summarizing their "highlights" of Title VI enforcement, an example of a complaint investigation was finding that a district was not racially discriminating in its adoption of a race-conscious admissions policy for a special program. Obama's OCR has also, in contrast with the Bush administration, helped to update existing desegregation cases to help districts meet their obligation to eliminate discrimination as circumstances change. This has meant, for example, working with a charter school that would have hampered a district's ability to desegregate, and ensuring that the building of new district schools aids desegregation efforts.

THE COURTS

In the immediate aftermath of *Parents Involved*, there were a few threats of litigation, which typically resulted in districts changing their policies. One of the first legal cases that occurred after *Parents Involved* was a challenge to redrawing high school boundaries in Lower Merion, Pennsylvania. Plaintiffs challenged the district because, as part of the boundary-drawing process, the district considered the demographics of neighborhoods they were seeking to reassign. One of the issues at stake in this case was what standard of review courts would use to judge the constitutionality of Lower Merion's actions. *Parents Involved* had been subject to strict scrutiny, which was the first time K–12 integration efforts had had to meet such a high bar to try to prove their constitutionality. Amicus briefs as well as the Department of Justice successfully argued that because no individual student's race/ethnicity was considered, a lesser standard of review should be used in the case.

The district court and Third Circuit Court agreed, and found the district's actions permissible. In a more recent decision, the Sixth Circuit also applied the lower standard of review for another redistricting plan, this time in Nashville, Tennessee. Nashville's rezoning plan replaced non contiguous zones— often used with busing to achieve more diverse schools—with choice zones and changes in busing. Blacks challenged the plan, arguing that it shuttled black students to more racially isolated schools. The district's plan was upheld, however, because it takes much less evidence under the lower standard of review to convince the court that the plan is a permissible consideration of race (in this case, the demographics of the zones that were able to take advantage of choice). As of this writing, the case has been appealed to the Supreme Court.

Thus, these two examples illustrate that the concern that after *Parents Involved* all race-conscious actions would be subject to heightened judicial scrutiny has not come to pass. However, they also show how a relaxed standard can make it easier for a district to implement a policy that may exacerbate segregation.

LOCAL DISTRICTS

At the local level, there have been a variety of ways that districts have responded to *Parents Involved* in terms of school integration. Some districts have dropped the pursuit of integration altogether while others have continued to pursue integration either with or without using race-conscious policies. Below, I describe some examples to illustrate the variability of approaches districts have taken.

One of the first legal challenges after *Parents Involved* was to the Specialized High School Institute in New York City that helps prepare students to take admissions tests required for admittance to the city's highly selective high schools in which black and Latino students are substantially underrepresented. After a conservative legal foundation filed a lawsuit on behalf of an Asian student who was excluded from attending the institute, the district switched from race-conscious selection process to one that targeted low-income students (McDermott, DeBray, and Frankenberg, 2012).

Two Illinois districts, each formerly operating under a desegregation consent decree, also ended their use of race-conscious student assignment policies after their consent decree ended, interpreting *Parents Involved* as forbidding the use of race. (Notably, these actions occurred prior to the release of the 2011 guidance outlining ways in which race could be used.) In Champaign, the district's consent decree ended in 2009 and they switched from the race-conscious controlled-choice plan they were using to a controlled-choice plan that considered a variety of socioeconomic factors in granting students' choices, along with preference for proximity. In Chicago, the parties in the desegregation case agreed to delay a unitary status hearing until after *Parents Involved* was released. In 2009, the consent decree ended, and the district removed the cap of 35 percent of white students in a magnet school (the district's enrollment is approximately 10 percent white). They also aimed to balance socioeconomic status and neighborhood residence in magnet school admissions. The district also promised to review whether these changes led to disproportionately high access for white students to magnet schools.

San Francisco is another example of a district that continues to pursue reducing racial isolation through race-neutral means. Its efforts are constrained by not only *Parents Involved* but also Proposition 209 in California, which restricted governmental use of race/ethnicity. Prior to *Parents Involved*, a federal court ended its oversight of SFUSD's student assignment plan, finding that the race-neutral diversity index had only made racial isolation worse. The district undertook an effort to simplify student assignment and make it more equitable, aided in part by receiving one of the TASAP grants. It adopted a new policy that gives students priority in choosing schools if they live in areas of the city that have historically been low achieving. It has also revised boundaries and created feeder patterns for middle schools to try to improve diversity and achievement.

There are a number of districts that have maintained or altered their voluntary integration policies in ways that still consider race as part of many factors in student assignment. Unlike the other defendant school district in *Parents Involved* that dropped its voluntary integration policy, Jefferson County (Louisville), Kentucky, has remained committed to race-conscious policies to pursue integration even in the face of legal and political challenges. Immediately after *Parents Involved*, the district declared its commitment to continue to pursue voluntary integration, and after a year of study, it adopted a multi-factor plan to assign students to schools. The plan defined diversity no longer solely using race but race in combination with adults' educational attainment and household income. In addition, the district considered the diversity of a region the child lived in, not simply the student's own background.

Challenged in both state and federal court, the plan has withstood all legal challenges. It has also been challenged in the community by school board candidates and the state legislature, but those challenges have also been unsuccessful.

In 2011, the district undertook consultation with experts to revise the plan to make it more effective, and has since adopted changes while retaining a multifaceted conception of diversity. The district's school board and leadership remains committed to this pursuit of integration.

One of the districts that Jefferson County modeled their plan after was Berkeley, California, which had adopted a multifactor integration plan that used race among several other demographic characteristics in 2004 due to California's Proposition 209. Berkeley successfully defended its plan in state court after *Parents Involved*, and has been fairly successful in creating racially diverse schools in a district with substantial racial residential segregation and inequality (Frankenberg, 2013a).

Another district that is using race-conscious policies to create diverse schools is Ector County ISD in Texas. Prior to the release of the federal guidance, the district's policy, which used seven factors in transfer and magnet school decisions, received approval from the federal government. Three of these factors were racial while others pertained to different socioeconomic characteristics (Siegel-Hawley and Frankenberg, 2011).

CONCLUSION

Pursuing integration has become legally—and in some cases politically—more challenging since *Parents Involved*. Yet, beyond the immediate aftermath of the decision, the federal government has signaled its support for districts to pursue integration and has outlined ways in which districts could effectively and legally do so. Further, several recent cases since *Parents Involved* have granted districts leniency in crafting student assignment policies even when they have considered race. The discussion of how local districts are implementing integration policies shows more reluctance to consider race, and it will be important to understand whether there is any tradeoff in effectiveness of race-neutral plans. Still, even if plans are less effective, they are likely better than not trying to create diverse schools altogether. Given the findings about the importance of diverse schools and the growing numbers of students of color, the federal government's support for integration will hopefully encourage other districts to devise student assignment policies according to their local context and needs that will seek to eliminate racial isolation—and continue to strive to fulfill the promise of *Brown v. Board of Education*.

REFERENCES

DeBray, E., K. A. McDermott, E. Frankenberg, and A. Blankenship. 2012, April. "Lessons from a Federal Grant for School Diversity: Tracing a Theory of Change and Implementation of Local Policies." Paper presented at the annual meeting of the American Educational Research Association, Vancouver, British Columbia.

Frankenberg, E. (2013a). "The Promise of Choice: Berkeley's Innovative Integration Plan." In *Educational Delusions? Why Choice Can Deepen Inequality and How to Make Schools Fair*, ed. G. Orfield, E. Frankenberg, et al. (pp. 69–88). Berkeley: University of California Press.

Frankenberg, E. 2013b. "The Role of Residential Segregation in Contemporary School Segregation." *Education and Urban Society* 45(5): 548–70. doi:10.1177/0013124513486288

Frankenberg, E., K. A. McDermott, E. DeBray, and A. Blankenship. 2012, April. "The Changing Politics of Diversity: Lessons from a Federal Technical Assistance Grant." Paper presented at the annual meeting of the American Educational Research Association, Vancouver, British Columbia.

Le, C. Q. 2010. Racially Integrated Education and the Role of the Federal Government. *North Carolina Law Review*, 88: 725–86.

McDermott, K., E. DeBray, and E. Frankenberg. 2012. "How Does *Parents Involved in Community Schools* Matter? Legal and Political Influence in Education Politics and Policy." *Teachers College Record* 114(12).

Orfield, G., J. Kucsera, and G. Siegel-Hawley. 2012. *E Pluribus Separated: A Diverse Society with Segregated Schools*. Los Angeles, CA: UCLA Civil Rights Project/ Proyecto Derechos Civiles.

Reardon, S., and J. T. Yun. 2005. Integrating Neighborhoods, Segregating Schools: The Retreat from School Desegregation in the South, 1990–2000. In *School*

Resegregation: Must the South Turn Back?, ed. J. C. Boger and G. Orfield (pp. 51–69). Chapel Hill: University of North Carolina Press.

Siegel-Hawley, G., and E. Frankenberg. 2011. Redefining Diversity: Political Responses to the Post-PICS Environment. *Peabody Journal of Education* 86(5): 529–52.

Chapter Nine

The Future of Detroit

How the City Got to Where It Is Now and What Is Next

Reynolds Farley

Every year a dozen or more books are published about Detroit, many of them describing the auto industry, the history of bitter racial conflict, the achievements of the city's sports teams, or how Detroit musicians influenced the nation's popular culture. In the last fifteen years, however, something new has emerged: coffee table books with numerous pictures of abandoned factories, dilapidated but once beautiful homes, and open areas that were once parks but are now weedy lots filled with abandoned trash (Moore 2010; Taubman 2012; Vergara 1995). Detroit enthusiasts call these books "ruin porn" since they capitalize upon the tragic status of many neighborhoods and industrial areas of Detroit to derive profits for photographers and publishers. Frequently these book include pictures of the people left behind, often bleak-looking individuals devoid of hope. Some—and similar expositions in art museums in the United States and Europe—primarily illustrate the photographer's ken in capturing the essence of urban abandonment and poverty. Even those who quickly scan the ruin porn literature will not be surprised to hear that the city's government approached destitution in 2012. The state legislature, in the last week of that year, hastily enacted a law that allowed the governor to appoint an official who could take over administration of the city. Governor Rick Snyder appointed Keyvn Orr as emergency manager of Detroit in March 2013, effectively minimizing the authority of elected officials in that city. After reviewing the city's finances, on July 18, 2013, Orr sought protection for the city from federal bankruptcy court.

What is the status of Detroit? Is it basically a wasteland with relics of an early twentieth-century industrial era—a few well-preserved but many in decay? Is it a location where modern factories produce steel, vehicles, and petroleum and where several vibrant medical centers employ thousands but much of the rest of the city contains the decaying homes and tumbledown factories that fill the pages of the ruin porn books? When David Bing became mayor of Detroit in 2010, he recognized the condition of many troubled neighborhoods and flirted with the idea of "downsizing." Many urban commentators praised this and presumed that "downsizing" would be a great start for Detroit. Is downsizing—either planned or produced by an exodus of residents who move to the suburbs—the inevitable fate of Detroit?

In this essay, I provide information about the current status of the city of Detroit, offer speculations about the most significant forces that produced the city that ruin porn photographs describe so graphically, and then provide information about the city's future. Large cities—especially ones with as many resources as Detroit—seldom die but they do change drastically.

At the outset, it is important to think about what we mean when we say Detroit. Is it the municipal government that sought Chapter 9 bankruptcy protection from the federal court in the summer of 2013? Is it the 701,000 people that the Census Bureau estimated were residents of the city in 2012? Or when you mention Detroit should you include the 167,000 persons who live in the suburbs but work in the city of Detroit, people who make use of city services and pay city income tax? What about the many people and prosperous firms that own property or run businesses in Detroit but live elsewhere? Is it the three to seven counties in southeast Michigan that comprise metropolitan Detroit, depending upon which definition you use? For the most part, I use Detroit to mean the 138 square miles in the municipality and those who live there. But I am aware that thousands more work in Detroit, have investments in the city, or frequently visit the city to enjoy its sports venues, casinos, museums, and restaurants. Where appropriate, I will present information about the three-county—Macomb, Oakland, and Wayne—metropolitan area, since the city and the suburbs are linked closely and are dependent upon each other.

DETROIT AT PRESENT: HOW DOES DETROIT COMPARE TO OTHER LARGE CITIES?

In a developed economy, population growth typically reflects an increase of employment but population increase is also a great stimulant for further economic growth. As Detroit became the Motor Capital, it was the fastest-growing large city in the United States in the first three decades of the twentieth century. By 1930, it was the fourth-largest city in the United States, trailing only New York, Chicago, and Philadelphia. During World War II, when Detroit served as the Arsenal of Democracy and allowed the Allies to defeat the German and Japanese military, its population undoubtedly exceeded two million, but the maximum census count was 1.85 million in 1950.

Detroit remained the nation's fourth-largest city until the late 1950s when it was surpassed by Los Angeles. And then, the federal government's housing and fiscal policies fostered an invasion of the crabgrass frontier. By 1950, Detroit's suburbs started to grow much more rapidly, while the city's population declined. Detroit's rank among the nation's cities also fell, to seventh largest in 1990 and to eighteenth in the most recent census.

Figure 9.1 shows the size of the twenty-five largest cities as estimated by the Census Bureau in 2012. Cities in the West—San Diego, San Jose, and Phoenix—have surpassed Detroit, as have a number of southern cities: Austin, Jacksonville, and Charlotte. And even two Midwestern cities: Columbus and Indianapolis are home to more residents than the Motor City. Nevertheless, Detroit in 2012 had a larger population than three states and the District of Columbia and a considerably larger population than such major cities as Atlanta, Boston, Denver, and Seattle.

Detroit differs from every other major city on most every important dimension. One of the most important is in the current trajectory of population change. Many cities in the South and West grew rapidly in the post–World War II era, often because they annexed the outlying fringe that would be a suburban ring in the Midwest. John Gallagher (2013, 7) reports that Dallas

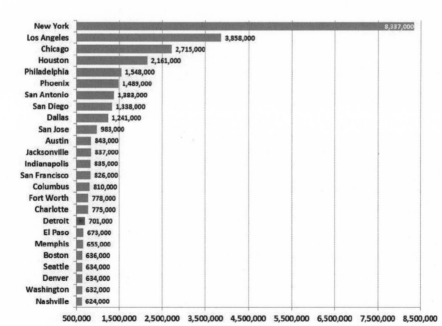

Figure 9.1.   Largest Cities in the United States in 2012 Ranked by Population Size

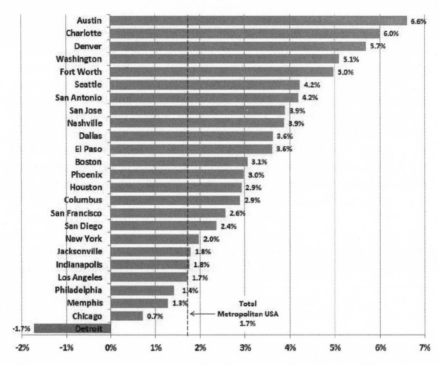

Figure 9.2. Largest Cities in 2012 Ranked by Percent Change in Population 2010 to 2012

grew from 112 square miles in 1950 to 340 at present, Houston from 160 square miles in 1950 to 600 square miles today. Had Detroit annexed the Macomb, Oakland, and Wayne suburban areas where homes were built in the 1950s, 1960s, and 1970s, the city would now be the third-largest in the nation. Detroit, however, last annexed outlying areas in 1926, and its size now is what it was ninety years ago. The city did not benefit at all, in population size, from the post–World War II growth boom. Many of the larger cities in the Northeast and Midwest reached their peak size in 1950 or 1960 and declined thereafter. Some of them reversed this trend in the 1990s and others in the first decade of this new century as downtown developments attracted young professionals working in city centers and other older neighborhoods were revived or reinvented. April 2010 was the date of the most recent national census. From that time until mid-2012, the population increased in twenty-four of the nation's twenty-five largest cities. Detroit was the sole city to lose residents, as indicated in figure 9.2. Austin and Charlotte grew by more than 6 percent in the early years of this decade. To be sure, Detroit's rate of population decline has slowed, but the influx of young people to downtown and midtown Detroit neighborhoods is not offsetting the substantial out-migration of many to the suburban ring. If the rates of population change shown in figure 9.2 were to persist for the remainder of this decade, all of the cities shown as smaller than Detroit will surpass the Motor City when Census 2020 is conducted, and Detroit will drop from the ranks of the top twenty-five.

Population decline is typically a challenge for the governance of a city, since it usually reflects a loss of jobs, a disinvestment in the city, and a rapidly declining tax base. Mayors and civic officials would much rather preside over the opening of new fire stations, shopping malls, factories, and schools than wrestle with how to lay off police officers, close parks, and shutter schools.

However, the demographic news about Detroit is much more unfavorable than just population decline. Compared to other large cities, Detroit's residents are not well educated, earn relatively little, and consequently suffer from high rates of poverty. They are also very much more likely to be victimized by crime than residents of other large cities.

The economic status of individuals—and cities—is strongly linked to educational attainment. The cities with the most prosperous populations, at present, are the cities whose inhabitants report the greatest educational attainments. Urban economists contend that the greatest asset of a city is the human capital of those who live or work there. That might be indexed by educational attainment. Figure 9.3 ranks cities in terms of the percent of the adult population that report a four-year college degree.

In Washington and San Francisco, more than a majority of adult residents completed college. In Austin, Denver, Boston, and San Diego, more than four in ten adults earned a degree. In Memphis, Philadelphia, and El Paso, the educational attainment levels were very much lower, but their residents had much greater human capital—as indicated by college attainment—than Detroit, where only 13 percent of adults had college diplomas. Across the nation, 31 percent of adults in metropolises had a four-year college degree. Detroit is quite distinct from all other major cities in the limited educational attainment of its residents.

Because of the lack of education, it comes as no surprise that Detroit's residents are not very economically successful. Two measures of economic status are reported here. Figure 9.4 ranks cities by per capita income at age twenty-one and over—that is, the pretax cash income reported by the typical resident as enumerated in the Census Bureau's American Community Survey. In Washington, the most prosperous of the large cities, per capita income approached $45,000. Seattle and San Francisco were municipalities where per capita adult income approached $40,000. San Jose is very similar to Detroit in that it has manufacturing as its economic base. But in San Jose,

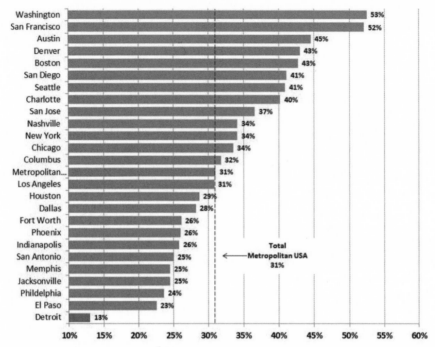

Figure 9.3.   Largest Cities in 2012 Ranked by Percent of Population Age Twenty-Five and Over with Four-Year College Degrees

the products are computers rather than vehicles. Residents of that large city reported per capita incomes of over $31,000. Detroit's per capita income falls far behind that of other large Midwestern cities at only $15,000. Indeed, the gaps are quite large. On a per capita basis, adults living in Chicago had $8,000 more to spend in a year than residents of Detroit; people in Columbus $7,000; and, perhaps surprisingly, even in Memphis per capita income was one-third larger than in Detroit.

El Paso is the only large city with income levels similar to those in Detroit. These income data may help to account for the dearth of retail stores in many neighborhoods of Detroit and for the low real estate values that surprise visitors.

Linked to low income is poverty, which is the second measure of economic standing. In 2012, the poverty line for a family of four was $23,300, meaning that any family of four with a pretax cash income below that line was considered impoverished. Poverty rates in large cities are generally higher than those in the suburban ring. Nevertheless, two large California cities—San

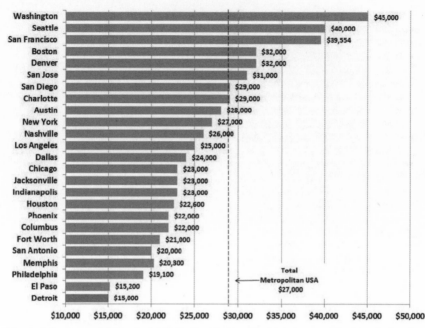

City	Income
Washington	$45,000
Seattle	$40,000
San Francisco	$39,554
Boston	$32,000
Denver	$32,000
San Jose	$31,000
San Diego	$29,000
Charlotte	$29,000
Austin	$28,000
New York	$27,000
Nashville	$26,000
Los Angeles	$25,000
Dallas	$24,000
Chicago	$23,000
Jacksonville	$23,000
Indianapolis	$23,000
Houston	$22,600
Phoenix	$22,000
Columbus	$22,000
Fort Worth	$21,000
San Antonio	$20,000
Memphis	$20,300
Philadelphia	$19,100
El Paso	$15,200
Detroit	$15,000

Total Metropolitan USA $27,000

$10,000 $15,000 $20,000 $25,000 $30,000 $35,000 $40,000 $45,000 $50,000

Figure 9.4. Largest Cities in 2012 Ranked by Per Capita Income of the Population Age Twenty-One and Over

Jose and San Francisco—had poverty rates below the national metropolitan average, as did Seattle. Other cities had poverty rates exceeding the national average, but Detroit, once again, was distinctive with an elevated poverty rate of 41 percent. Philadelphia was the city with a poverty rate closest to that of Detroit, but the poverty rate there—28 percent—was much lower than Detroit's.

The poverty rate in Detroit was about two and one-half times the national average. It is important to consider the poverty rate of the total population but, in term of consequences for the next generation, it is useful to think about the poverty rate of persons under age eighteen. In Detroit, the Census Bureau's most recent survey estimated that 54 percent of the preschool and school-age population lived in households with incomes below the poverty line; that is, the majority of children in Detroit live in impoverished households. At the other extreme, in San Francisco, only 16 percent of children were impoverished.

Tax revenues to support a municipality depend, to a substantial degree, upon the value of homes and buildings. There are many sources to support a local government but, in most places, property taxes are a key component. Detroit is different from many cities in that property taxes now account for

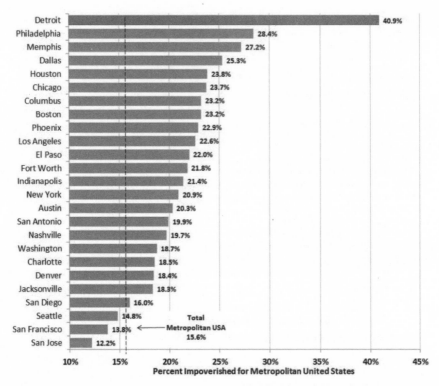

Figure 9.5.   Largest Cities Ranked by Percent of Population Impoverished

only 24 percent of general fund tax revenue. Given the population losses in Detroit and the weak economic status of its residents, it comes as no shock to find that the city's property tax base is limited. Figure 9.6 provides information about this by showing the median value of owner-occupied homes or condominiums in the nation's largest cities. This is not the sales price of recent transactions but rather the owner's assessment of his or her residence's worth were it to be sold.

The nation's real estate market varies greatly from one location to another but is strongly influenced by the economic conditions, population growth, and zoning regulations in an area. Single-family homes or condominiums have a median value in excess of $700,000 in San Francisco and more than $500,000 in San Jose. That may not be a surprise. But in large cities that have grown slowly and are not at the foci for new high-tech industries or the financial sector—Jacksonville, El Paso, and Indianapolis—typical homes are worth two and one-half or three times what homes are valued at in Detroit.

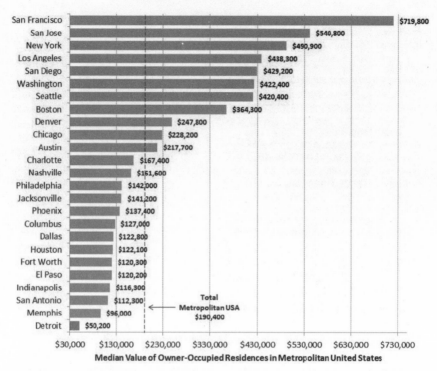

Figure 9.6. Largest Cities in the United States Ranked by Median Value of Owner-Occupied Homes

Memphis is closest to Detroit in value of homes, but in Tennessee city homes are worth, on average, roughly twice what homes are worth in Detroit.

Linked to depressed housing values in Detroit is the vacancy problem. Detroit's population fell by 64 percent from 1950 to 2012, but the stock of housing did not contract at nearly that rate so Detroit leads the nation in number of abandoned structures. Figure 9.7 ranks the nation's largest cities by the percent of their housing stock vacant. Some of these vacant units may be new ones awaiting their first renters or owners but, in Detroit, almost all of them were occupied in prosperous years during and just after World War II but are now empty due to the exodus of population. Quite likely they will remain empty. About 30 percent of the housing units enumerated by the Census Bureau in the American Community Survey were vacant. That is, when the Census Bureau surveyed Detroit in 2011, they found 264,000 occupied residential units and 99,000 vacant ones. Memphis, Jacksonville, and Chicago were next on the list but, in those places, about 15 percent of the homes were

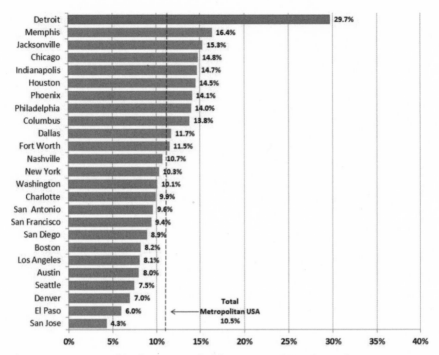

Figure 9.7.   Largest Cities in 2012 Ranked by Percent of Housing Units Vacant

vacant. And in the cities that have grown rapidly in recent years, the vacancy rate was far below the national average of 11 percent.

Given the trend toward rapidly declining property values, Detroit's government sought other sources of revenue. Detroit is one of twenty-two Michigan cities imposing an income tax on its residents and that is now the largest source of general fund revenue. Detroit is the only Michigan city to tax casino gambling revenues and that source now supplies 30 percent of general fund revenues. Detroit is the only city in the state to add a tax to every utility bill.

Not only is Detroit home to a population with a limited educational attainment and rather little income, it is also distinctive for its high crime rate. The Federal Bureau of Investigation attempts to assemble comparable crime rates on a prompt basis. Figure 9.8 shows the same array of cities ranked in terms of reported violent crimes per 100,000 residents in 2011. Violent crimes include murder, non-negligent manslaughter, forcible rape, robbery, and aggravated assault. San Jose, San Diego, and Austin reported the lowest incidence of violent crime, with fewer than 400 such crimes per 100,000 resi-

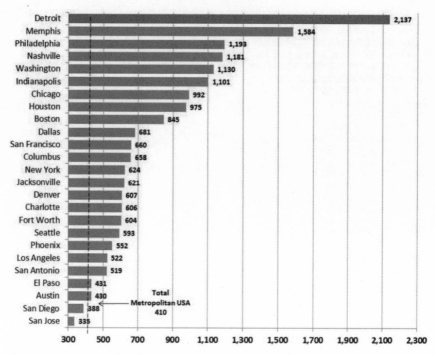

Figure 9.8. Largest Cities in 2012 Ranked by Violent Crimes per 100,000

dents. Detroit was at the other extreme with 2,100 violent crimes per 100,000. That was a considerably higher rate than the next city—Memphis—and more than five times the national metropolitan average for violent crime. The violent crime rate in Chicago was only 46 percent as great as in Detroit; in New York, 28 percent as great.

Perhaps, not surprisingly, Detroit also has the highest murder rate of any of the twenty-five largest cities as illustrated in Figure 9.9. The murder rate in Detroit has declined irregularly and slowly since a peak in the 1970s, but 344 murders were reported in 2011 implying a murder rate of 48 per 100,000. That is much more than double the murder rate in the second-ranked city—Philadelphia—and more than three times the rate in Chicago. There are large cities where murders are infrequent compared to Detroit. San Diego, with a population almost twice the size of Detroit, recorded only 38 murders in 2011, Austin 28, and Seattle 20. El Paso's population is just a bit smaller than that of Detroit but, in 2011, only 16 persons were murdered there.

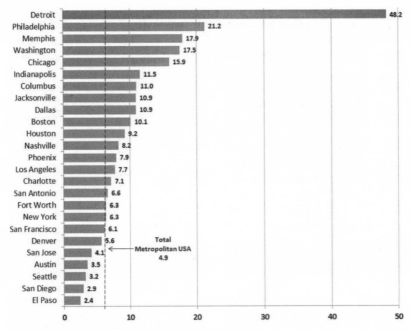

Figure 9.9.   Largest Cities in 2012 Ranked by Murders per 100,000

WHY IS DETROIT DIFFERENT FROM OTHER LARGE CITIES?

The Michigan System of Local Governance

Three major reasons explain why Detroit differs from other large cities and why it faced bankruptcy in 2013. Other municipalities share many of Detroit's problems, but their populations are more highly educated and more prosperous. And the housing stock in other cities provides a much more solid tax base than does the housing stock in Detroit. The first reason is the organization of local government in Michigan. As the state's population changed from primarily rural in the nineteenth century to predominantly urban in the early twentieth, the legislature adopted a Home Rule law in 1911 and then amended it many times. This legislation greatly facilitated the process whereby villages, small settlements, and townships could become independent cities. Then it empowered those cities to levy taxes and maintain municipal services. This law, and others, eventually came to strongly discourage annexation or mergers. Once incorporated, a municipality could easily fend off annexation attempts by contiguous municipalities. The Michigan Home Rule Law facilitated the creation of dozens of new suburban cities close to

Detroit. At present, the city of Detroit is surrounded by 158 other separate and distinct municipalities: 68 in Wayne County, 62 in Oakland County, and 28 in Macomb County. After World War II, federal housing policies encouraged the building of new homes by making mortgages available at low cost to moderate-income families and veterans regardless of their earnings. Large stretches of the northern area of the city of Detroit had been platted for development in the 1920s but then the Depression terminated new construction. If you visit these areas today, you see that they were filled in by modest workingmen's homes in the immediate post–World War II years. By 1950, however, Detroit's huge land area was almost completely occupied. Federal housing policies encouraged the invasion of the vast crabgrass frontier in Macomb, Oakland, and Wayne counties.

Michigan's Home Rule law provided municipalities with few, if any, incentives to cooperate with each other. Just the opposite, cities competed with each other for residential developments, employment centers, and shopping malls as each place sought to maximize its tax base. Transportation systems, economic development, park systems, and postsecondary schools are programs that serve large numbers of people from all corners of a metropolitan area. They would benefit from cooperation among neighboring cities. Indeed, you might even expect there would be some metropolitan-wide taxes levied to fund these services that support and improve the quality of life for all residents of a metropolis. No such taxes are imposed in Michigan, and cities in metropolitan Detroit continue to provide most of their own services. Every municipality in Michigan is dependent upon the tax revenue it raises, typically from taxing property.

The Home Rule system of governance, although far from ideal, may function adequately if there is continuous population and economic growth. If that occurs, most municipalities will, year after year, have more homes and business to tax, although some places will do much better than others. From 1940 to about 1970, Michigan was a state of great employment and population growth. The number of employed residents in Michigan rose from 1.9 million in 1940 to 2.5 million in 1950 and then to 3.3 million in 1970. The twenty-five years after World War II were excellent ones for the state, marked by steady increases in jobs and a secular trend toward much higher wage rates. The state's population, encouraged by both the tremendous economic expansion and the unforeseen baby boom, rose from 5.2 million at the start of World War II to 8.9 million in 1970.

Population and economic growth in Michigan reached a major turning point in the early 1970s. The embargo of the oil producing nations helped propel a change in the way manufacturing industries operated in the United States. Those firms, facing great competition, were driven to use much more efficient production processes and to shift production to low-wage areas in the United States or abroad. Michigan, being a high-wage state, did not fare well in this completion. Employment in Michigan in 2013 is at 4.2 million, very close to the number employed twenty-five years ago. The postwar baby boom ended late in the 1960s, contributing to a slowdown in population growth. After the end of the baby boom, social values changed and women entered both colleges and the labor force in great numbers. Michigan shifted to become a state with replacement-level fertility and, more recently, to below-replacement fertility. In brief, there has been very little increase in population in the last forty years and no more than modest growth of employment, primarily attributable to women joining the labor force. Since the late 1990s, Michigan has had a near constant population of 9.9 million.

There is nothing in Michigan law that encourages Michigan cities to face the severe consequences of population and economic decline. No governor has appointed a committee to design a program to cope with the state's population and economic stagnation. Indeed, I believe there was—and may still be—a widespread belief that the tremendous industrial restructuring that began in the 1970s in Michigan and the sharp downturn in population growth that occurred shortly thereafter were temporary aberrations and that the favorable trends of the post–World War II era will return. Michigan's Home Rule system works poorly in an era of economic and population stagnation or decline.

Detroit, arguably, led the nation in the loss of population to its suburban ring in the 1950s, 1960s, and 1970s. Figure 9.10 shows the decade-by-decade change in the number of white and black residents in the city and in the suburban ring. These are net change numbers, so they reflect migration but they are also influenced by births and deaths. Because race has been such a divisive issue in the metropolis, data are shown for the two races.

In both the 1950s and 1960s, the white population of Detroit decreased by more than one-third of a million; in the 1970s, by an even larger figure. The white population of the city continues to sink but by smaller numbers. Until the 1970s, Detroit attracted African American migrants, primarily from the South, but the post–World War II gains in black population did not offset the loss of whites, so the city's population got smaller and smaller. Beginning in the 1990s, there was an out-migration of blacks, so the city-to-suburb migration that was typical for Detroit's white residents decades ago is now occurring among African Americans. As a result of these demographic trends, Detroit residents comprise a smaller and smaller share of the metropolitan population. Figure 9.11 shows the percent of total, white, and black metropolitan population living in the city. Detroit's share of the metropolitan population declined from 69 percent in 1940 to 18 percent in 2011. As shown,

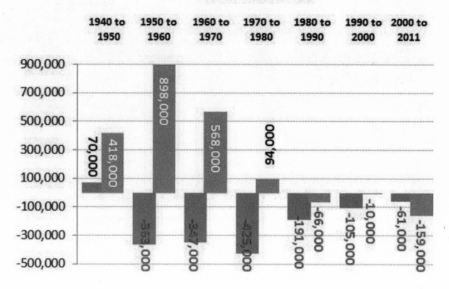

WHITE POPULATION

| 1940 to 1950 | 1950 to 1960 | 1960 to 1970 | 1970 to 1980 | 1980 to 1990 | 1990 to 2000 | 2000 to 2011 |

- 70,000
- 418,000
- 898,000
- -363,000
- -347,000
- 568,000
- -425,000
- 94,000
- -191,000
- -66,000
- -105,000
- -10,000
- -61,000
- -159,000

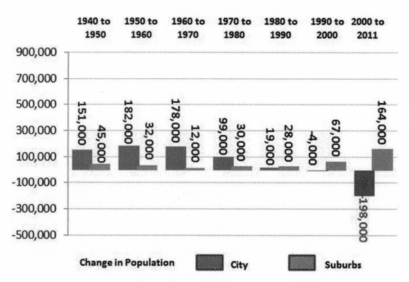

BLACK POPULATION

| 1940 to 1950 | 1950 to 1960 | 1960 to 1970 | 1970 to 1980 | 1980 to 1990 | 1990 to 2000 | 2000 to 2011 |

- 151,000
- 45,000
- 182,000
- 32,000
- 178,000
- 12,000
- 99,000
- 30,000
- 19,000
- 28,000
- -4,000
- 67,000
- -198,000
- 164,000

Change in Population   ■ City   ■ Suburbs

Figure 9.10.   Changes in the White and Black Population in the City of Detroit and in the Three-County Suburban Ring: 1940 to 2011

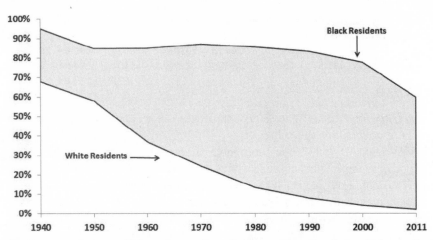

Figure 9.11. Percent of Three-County Detroit Metropolitan Population Living in the City of Detroit: 1940 to 2011

the white share of metropolitan population living in the city of Detroit fell to 2 percent. The current suburbanization process is reducing the city's share of the metropolitan black population and it is possible that the next census will show the majority of the local African American population lives in the suburbs.

In recent decades the city of Detroit lost much of its tax base. The population paying property taxes fell sharply, the value of homes declined as many were abandoned and many of the once vibrant industrial plants that lined the city's rail lines and highways were closed. The city's population and employment continues to decline, so fewer and fewer pay income tax. People who live and work in the city of Detroit, now are obligated to pay 2.4 percent of their income to the city while those who live outside the city but work in the city pay 1.2 percent. Between 2000 and 2011, the constant dollar earnings of those who live and work in Detroit fell by 49 percent. The earnings of those who commute to jobs in Detroit fell by 25 percent, reflecting fewer jobs in the city and lower wages. Given the tremendous declines in employment and taxable property in Detroit, the July 2013 bankruptcy was not surprising.

To be sure, there are locations of economic growth in the city of Detroit—downtown, midtown and along the east riverfront. But many of the employers that have grown in recent years are nonprofit hospitals or Wayne State University, which pay no or small property taxes. And while there have been major new investments in some industrial sites, including the Marathon Oil refinery in southwest Detroit and the Jefferson North plant of Chrysler-Fiat, it is now common for local governments to offer them a substantial tax abatement in exchange for their investment. These for-profit firms pay substantial property taxes but they also benefit from abatements. The tax base of the city has contracted more rapidly than its population, but the obligation of the city's government to provide services has, apparently, not contracted in tandem. The city of Detroit is home to about 18 percent of the three-county population but contains only 6 percent of the area's taxable property (Gallagher 2013, 15). The problems of a declining tax base leading to an inability to finance governmental services are not unique to Detroit. Several of the older suburbs faced fiscal challenges and could no longer pay for their services. Six Detroit suburbs were in such precarious status that governors appointed an emergency manager who controlled or controls all municipal spending: Allen Park (since October, 2012), Ecorse (since October, 2009), and Hamtramck (twice, most recently since March, 2013), Highland Park (2001 but now solvent), Inkster (since February 2012), and Pontiac (since March 2009).

Several decisions could have averted the problem of Detroit's lacking resources to support the municipal government it needs. More than half of the cities that surpassed Detroit in population after the end of World War II annexed outlying areas that would have been their suburban ring. If Detroit had been able to merge with or annex some inner-ring and outer-ring suburbs in the 1960s and 1970s, it might now be much stronger economically. Or, if civic and political leaders had realized that most issues that now affect residents' well-being and prosperity are primarily metropolitan in scope, they could have developed revenue-sharing programs or joint taxation measures to promote economic growth, environmental improvements, efficient transportation, and appealing parks. Unfortunately those opportunities were missed in Michigan and individual municipalities continue to compete with each other. The challenges that cities face have greatly changed because of improved transportation and better communication, but the system of local government remains what it was a century ago.

Race and Racial Conflicts: Their Implications for Explaining the Current Status of Detroit

Racial issues are the second reason for the unique status of Detroit. It is the only city where federal troops have been dispatched to the streets four times to prevent black and white residents from killing each other: twice in the nineteenth century—once in the era of slavery and again during the Civil War—and twice in the twentieth—during World War II and again in the Civil Rights decade. The 1967 rioting in Detroit from July 23 to July 26 was more violent than other contemporaneous violence, leaving forty-three dead. After that bloodshed, President Johnson appointed Illinois Governor Otto Kerner to chair a committee to investigate the causes of urban racial rioting and suggest strategies to end urban racial violence. The committee emphasized the disparity of opportunities for blacks and whites in the nation's cities, especially inequalities in opportunities for employment and education. They also stressed the consistent mistreatment of blacks in their encounters with the police and civic authorities. The Kerner Commission's most cited conclusion was that if current trends persisted, the nation would soon come to have central cities with largely minority and lower income residents surrounded by suburbs that were overwhelmingly white and much more prosperous—a kind of American Apartheid to use the vividly descriptive term of Douglas Massey and Nancy Denton (1993).

Fortunately, the Kerner Commission was wrong about most metropolises. They did not foresee the arrival of millions of immigrants from abroad who often settled in older inner-city neighborhoods, reviving areas that had lost their white populations to the suburbs. Nor did the Kerner Commission foresee the remarkable increases in employment in the medical sector, financial services, and higher education; industries which are generally located in central cities. But the Kerner Commission was correct about Detroit. This is not surprising, since they were strongly influenced by the racial conflicts in the Motor City that provoked the 1967 violence.

It would be easy to develop a convincing argument that race is the key issue that explains the decline of population in Detroit, the exodus of economic activity from the city, the reduction in manufacturing jobs, and the bankruptcy request filed by Emergency Manager Orr. But it would be equally easy to convincingly argue that Detroit's population would have plummeted after 1950 and that its economic problems today would be severe had it been a mono-racial city at the end of World War II. A careful and thorough analysis, I believe, leads to the conclusion that Detroit is different from other cities and metropolises because of the way racial polarization occurred within an ineffective system of local government. And after Detroit became an overwhelming African American municipality, lack of employment opportunities began to greatly disadvantage and impoverish blacks.

Blacks first began coming to Detroit in large numbers during World War I after the German navy blocked the immigration of eastern Europeans needed to staff the vehicle factories that had become defense plants. A very small number of African Americans worked in the professions before World War I and a larger—but still small—number of low-income ones shared near East Side neighborhoods with German, Italian and Eastern European immigration. But with the arrival of many blacks in Detroit during the Great War, the Jim Crow system of segregation was quickly imported from the American South and influenced almost all elements of city life even though it was seldom enforced by Michigan law.

Basically, blacks found themselves restricted in the jobs they could hold, in where they could live, and which public accommodations they might enjoy. To be sure, jobs were readily available for black men during the World War I era and the booming 1920s, but blacks did not have access to higher-skilled jobs and black women were pretty much restricted to domestic service. Civil rights groups quickly emerged in Detroit. Some fought against segregation and eventually won victories such as the public school system hiring blacks to teach in secondary schools in the mid-1930s and the fire department appointing black firefighters late in that decade. Other black organizations in Detroit followed the lead of Booker T. Washington and sought to expand employment opportunities, albeit on a segregated basis. For example, a system of black proprietary hospitals developed and contributed to the city's Jim Crow health system. There were differences from the American South since street cars were not segregated and blacks could vote. Indeed, the votes of Detroit blacks in 1925 helped to defeat Charles Bowles, a Ku Klux Klan candidate running for mayor. A thorough system of racial segregation emerged in Detroit's public schools but it was on a de facto not de jure basis.

The 1940s brought about change. Jobs were readily available because of World War II. A. Philip Randolph and other African American leaders succeeded in getting President Roosevelt to issue Executive Order # 8802 on June 25, 1941, banning racial discrimination in employment and requiring equal pay and promotions for blacks and whites in defense industries. This order may have had a greater impact on Detroit than in any other city. But in Detroit's defense plants, it provoked prolonged and bitter racial hate strikes— whites walking off the job if blacks were promoted to skilled jobs or supervisory positions and blacks walking off the job if they were not promoted. Federal government labor agents put down most of these strikes without resort to force, but this employment conflict played a role in the racial violence that began on the Belle Isle Bridge on Sunday evening, June 20, 1943—the largest of World War II, and one that caused the deaths of thirty-four Motor City residents. It was effectively brought under control when President Roosevelt ordered the Fifth Army to Detroit on the evening of July 21.

After World War II, President Truman prodded Congress to enact a law for fair employment practices, but they refused to do so. Many believed that after a brief post–World War II boom, economic conditions would deteriorate and sink back to the dismal levels of the Depression. White workers in Detroit had strong incentive to protect their interests by keeping blacks out of skilled jobs and supervisory positions, a process strongly opposed by Detroit's vibrant civil rights organizations. But the economy boomed in the years after World War II and there was something of a labor shortage in the area. The major post–World War II conflict was over residential space. The idea that neighborhoods with black residents were unfit places for whites to live had a history dating back to the early years of the twentieth century. Supposedly, the arrival of blacks would lead to much higher crime rates, a drastic decline in the quality of schools, plummeting property values and would put white women at risk of violence. Many Detroit area blacks had the financial resources to live in those higher-quality neighborhoods that were appropriate for their status.

Blacks, during World War II, had been effectively confined to a few clearly delineated and well-known neighborhoods: the traditional east- and west-side ghettos and a couple of other pockets in the city, including Conant Gardens and an area south of Eight Mile and west of Wyoming. Thomas Sugrue (1996) lucidly describes the major conflicts that occurred in many Detroit neighborhoods as blacks sought to purchase homes but whites, often with the help of policies such as those calling for redlining, attempted to preserve the "racial purity" of their areas. For the most part whites delayed, but did not succeed in stopping, the invasion of African Americans seeking better housing.

Whites left the city in massive numbers as shown in figure 9.10. It would be erroneous to assume that race was the only or even the most important factor in that exodus. Federal housing policies encouraged the building of new homes and made them available at low cost. Within a decade and a half after World War II, consumers' taste about housing changed. The small workingman's bungalow was no longer popular. People wanted larger homes with separate bedrooms for each of their children, desired two-car garages attached to their homes to protect them from rough winter weather, expected homes to be air-conditioned, and wanted a reasonably large lot to provide privacy, space for children to play, and a garden. Few homes in the city of Detroit offered such amenities. The many homes built in the city after World War II were very small on tiny lots and lacked the popular amenities. Remodeling the more expensive older homes in Detroit to provide the amenities was costly. The "aged" housing stock of Detroit explains much of the exodus as residents who could afford to leave for the suburbs did so: first whites and now African Americans.

In the Detroit area and in many other Midwest and northern metropolises, suburban communities effectively excluded blacks. Real estate brokers would not sell to and bankers—backed up by the federal redlining policies—would not loan to blacks who sought suburban housing, except in a handful of Detroit suburbs where black enclaves had been established before World War II. Mayor Orville Hubbard of Dearborn became a well-known national spokesman for the widely adopted practice of excluding blacks from suburbs. As a result of these demographic trends and racial policies, by 1980 the city of Detroit with its 1.2 million residents was approaching two-thirds African

American but in the suburban ring only 4 percent of the 3.1 million residents were black—most of those living in Pontiac, Inkster, Royal Oak Township, and a few other enclaves. At that time—more than thirty years ago—there was already a great city-suburb discrepancy in economic status. One-fifth of the city's population but only 6 percent in the suburbs lived in impoverished households. The Kerner Commission accurately projected what would happen in Detroit.

Persistent practices of residential segregation produced a city of Detroit that is different from other large cities in its lack of racial diversity. Although the black population of Detroit is now rapidly declining, the white population is also getting smaller, so the proportion of African Americans in the city rose to 83 percent in 2011.

Figure 9.12 shows a measure of racial diversity for the largest twenty-five cities. Using data from the Census Bureau's *American Community Survey*, all residents have been classified into one of eight distinct racial categories: white, black, Asian, American Indian, Pacific Islander; Hispanic, two or more races, and some other race. The index reported in this figure shows what

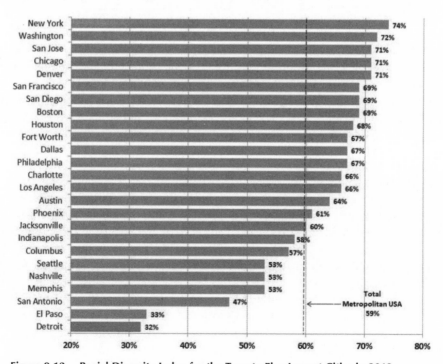

Figure 9.12.   Racial Diversity Index for the Twenty-Five Largest Cities in 2012

would happen if you randomly selected two residents of the city. It indicates
the percent of time that those two individuals would represent different races.
Many—or most—of the nation's large cities have benefitted from international migration in recent decades, so they have diverse populations. The
stream of those arriving from abroad is bimodal in terms of educational credentials: many individuals with extensive educations and advanced degrees
and many others with few years of classroom education. In most cities, the
extensively educated take jobs in science, technology, and in the financial
services and medical sectors. Those immigrants with limited educations often
fill jobs Americans are reluctant to accept: household service, yard maintenance, and the lower-skilled blue-collar jobs. And in many of the large cities,
immigrants with limited incomes have stabilized and revitalized older neighborhoods whose housing stock appeals to few Americans.

If you randomly selected two residents of New York City, 74 percent of the
time they would differ in race; in Washington, 72 percent would come from
different races, and 69 percent of the time that would happen in Boston. Detroit is different because of its predominantly African American population.
Only 32 percent of the time would two randomly selected residents of Detroit
differ in race. To be sure, El Paso has a diversity index close to that of Detroit
since 80 percent of its residents are Hispanics, primarily from Mexico.

Detroit—and Michigan—have largely missed out on the stimulating effects that international migration often provides for economic growth and
neighborhood revitalization in the forty-five years since the nation's immigration laws were liberalized. Indeed, Detroit is distinctive for the very small
number of immigrants who have arrived in recent years. Figure 9.13 shows
the percent foreign born for the nation's largest cities in 2012.

In the West Coast cities of San Francisco, San Jose, and Los Angeles, and
in New York City, about four residents in ten were immigrants from abroad.
Overall, slightly more than one-sixth of the nation's metropolitan residents reported foreign birthplaces. Detroit was different. The city has attracted few immigrants in recent decades, so only one resident in twenty was an immigrant.

Something of a *Hispanification* of the United States has occurred in recent
decades. Between Census 2000 and Census 2010, the Spanish-origin population of the nation grew by 44 percent. Detroit did not share in that growth, so
the city was exceptional when compared to most other places since census
2000 and 2010 counted very nearly the same number of Hispanics in Detroit. To be sure, there is a vibrant Hispanic community residing in the older
workingmen's homes in southwest Detroit and shopping in many stores along
Vernor Highway. But it is one of the nation's few Hispanic communities that
has not grown recently.

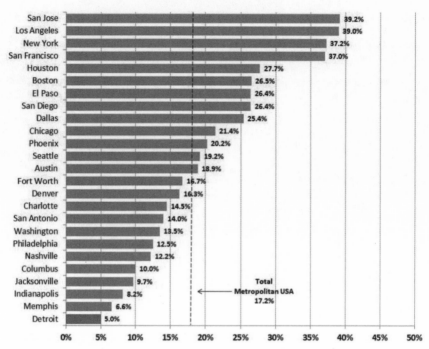

Figure 9.13. Largest Cities in 2012 Ranked by Percent of Population Born Outside the United States

The Civil Rights Revolution and the encompassing laws of the 1960s have had a great and positive effect. Racial attitudes changed. Schools and neighborhoods are somewhat more racially integrated now than in the past, and blacks are increasingly represented in the most rewarding professions. I have had the opportunity to monitor one aspect of that change, namely the changing views of Detroit area whites about neighborhood integration.

In 1976, 1992, and 2004 my colleagues and I at the University of Michigan conducted surveys to determine whites' beliefs and values about residential integration. We measured whether whites felt comfortable living with black neighbors, whether they would remain in their neighborhoods when blacks moved in, and whether whites were willing to consider moving to neighborhoods where blacks already resided. In each survey, we gave white respondents five cards showing neighborhoods with racial compositions ranging from all white to half white and half black. We told them to imagine they lived in an all-white neighborhood similar to the first card shown in figure 9.14. For many whites this was a realistic assumption. We then gave them a

Figure 9.14. Neighborhood Cards for White Respondents

card showing a minimally integrated neighborhood—one black family and fourteen white. This is the second card displayed in this illustration.

We asked them whether they would be uncomfortable should their own neighborhood come to resemble the neighborhood shown on the second card. If they said they would feel comfortable living in that neighborhood, we presented them with the third card, showing more black residents in their neighborhood. Once again, we asked if they would feel comfortable should their neighborhood resemble the one shown on the card. We continued showing neighborhood cards until the white respondent either said he or she would feel uncomfortable or they came to the final card showing a neighborhood with eight black and seven white families. If a person said they would feel uncomfortable in a neighborhood, we asked if they would try to move away. The 1976, 1992, and 2004 surveys used identical questions with randomly selected respondents in the three-county metropolis.

The views of Detroit-area whites have changed greatly since the 1970s: they are much more accepting of African American neighbors. Figure 9.15 below summarizes the increasing willingness of whites to share neighborhoods with blacks.

Increasing proportions of whites report they feel comfortable with African American neighbors. In 1976, three-quarters of whites said they would feel comfortable if their neighborhood had just one black family. In 2004, whites almost universally accepted that minimum level of integration: 93 percent

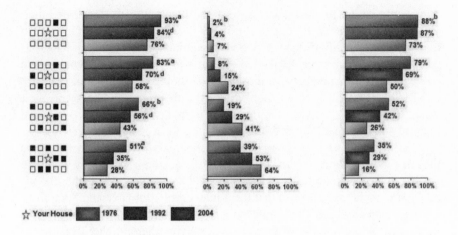

☆ Your House ■ 1976 ■ 1992 ■ 2004

Note: Sample size was 379 in 1976; 736 in 1992 and 330 in 2004.
a. Percent in 2004 differs significantly from percents in 1992 and 1976.
b. Percent in 2004 differs significantly from percent in 1976, but not from percent in 1992.
d. Percent in 1992 differs significantly from percent in 1976.

Figure 9.15. Attractiveness of Neighborhoods of Varying Racial Compositions for White Respondents; 1976, 1992, and 2004

were comfortable with one black in their neighborhood. Race, however, made a difference in the way whites feel. In all years, the comfort level of whites decreased as the number of their black neighbors went up. In 2004, two-thirds of whites said they would feel comfortable living in a five-black, ten-white neighborhood, but when we got to an eight-black, seven-white neighborhood whites were split fifty-fifty with regard to comfort. Nevertheless, that was a sharp shift since 1976, when only one white in four would be comfortable in the eight-black, seven-white neighborhood.

The story of neighborhood change in the city of Detroit after World War II was white flight. Blacks entered neighborhoods as whites departed. Chicago alderman Francis Lawler defined integration as that interval between the arrival of the first black and the departure of the last white. For many Detroit neighborhoods, that was a short time. White attitudes about moving away when African Americans arrive changed substantially. They are now much more willing to stay. In 1976, 40 percent of whites said they would try to move away if their neighborhood came to have a composition that included ten white and five black families, but that is no longer the case. In 2004, only 19 percent of whites said they would try to move away when their neighborhood became one-third black. Indeed, the majority of whites in 2004 said they would not try to move away even if blacks numerically dominated their neighborhood. Back in 1976, two-thirds of whites said they would have tried to move out. White flight may now be less common than in the past but it has probably not ended, since 39 percent of whites in 2004 said they would try to move away if their neighborhood tipped over the fifty-fifty balance.

After asking whites about their comfort with black neighbors and their desire to move out, we gave the five cards to them a second time. We asked them to suppose that they had been searching for a new home and found a nice, affordable one in each of the neighborhoods portrayed on the cards they had in their hands. We asked which of the neighborhoods they would be willing to move into. All that the respondent knew is that the neighborhoods differed in racial makeup and that the homes were affordable and attractive.

At all dates, whites' willingness to enter a neighborhood was strongly influenced by the number of blacks already living there: higher densities of blacks meant fewer whites would consider that location for their new home. Almost all whites reported they were willing to move into a neighborhood that was minimally integrated with just one black family. When you get to three black families in the neighborhood, the overwhelming majority of whites—about 80 percent—in 2004 would consider it but one-fifth would rule it out because of its racial makeup.

The fourth card showed a neighborhood with an even higher density of blacks—one-third black. In 1976 one-quarter of whites said they would consider a nice, affordable home in such a place. This rose to over a majority of whites in 2004. In 1976, only 16 percent said they would consider an attractive, affordable home in a neighborhood that was majority black but with numerous white families living there. White attitudes about moving into such neighborhoods changed: 35 percent in 2004 were willing to consider an attractive, affordable home in the eight-black, seven-white neighborhood.

When whites seek new homes they devote attention to the racial composition of the neighborhood. If blacks are there in modest numbers, most Detroit area whites are willing to consider the place, but as the percent black goes up, whites' willingness to consider the neighborhood goes down. Our major conclusion is that whites' attitudes about living with blacks changed greatly, since they were significantly more accepting of black neighbors in 2004 than in 1976.

There has been considerable social integration of whites and blacks in metropolitan America, including Detroit. To be sure, residential segregation is still the norm, but census data reveal an important decline in the residential isolation of blacks and whites. Demographers typically use census data and the index of dissimilarity to measure residential segregation. This index would equal 100 were there a system of apartheid so severe that all whites lived in exclusively white neighborhoods and all blacks in exclusively white neighborhoods. In 1980 this index, when calculated for metropolitan Detroit was 88, meaning that 88 percent of either black or white residents would have to move from their neighborhood to a different one to eliminate residential segregation. By 2010, that index had decreased to 74. Detroit is still one of the more segregated metropolises, but the degree of segregation is now substantially lower than in the past. This is largely due to the suburbanization of blacks.

When the movement of blacks from the city to the suburbs started in the late 1980s or early 1990s, demographers speculated that central-city black neighborhoods would cross the city-suburban border and new suburban ghettos would emerge close to the central city. That has not happened in metropolitan Detroit. Instead, almost all of the suburban communities—even those that had a reputation for great hostility to blacks, including Dearborn, Warren, Macomb County, and the Grosse Pointes—now have modest and growing African American populations.

Increasing interracial marriage is another indicator of the social integration of the races occurring in the Detroit area. Most married people aged twenty-five to thirty-four wedded within the last ten years. In 1970, only 1 percent of young black married men in metropolitan Detroit had wives that were white. This changed and, in 2012, 10 percent of young black married men in metropolitan Detroit had white wives. There has been an increase, but much smaller, in the percent of white men with black wives. As a result, the interracial population of metropolitan Detroit is growing. By 2011, 5 percent of the children under age ten in metropolitan Detroit were reported by their parents to be multiracial children. The most common multiracial children in metropolitan Detroit have one white and one black parent.

Gradually, social integration is occurring in metropolitan Detroit as blacks and whites increasingly live in the same neighborhoods and marry each other, undoubtedly a consequence of the many changes produced in the civil rights decade. A much less favorable trend occurred with regard to economic changes. On almost all key indicators, blacks are further behind whites now than they were in 1970. Employment differences, earnings differences, and differences in median household income have, with few exceptions, grown larger.

Except in times of great economic crisis, we would expect that most men age twenty-five to fifty-nine would report themselves as holding a job when the census taker or survey person called to ask about their labor force status. For women, we would expect gradual increases over time in the percent holding a job. Figure 9.16 considers white and black adult men and women in metropolitan Detroit from 1970 to 2011 and shows the percent who reported that they were employed.

DATA FOR WOMEN

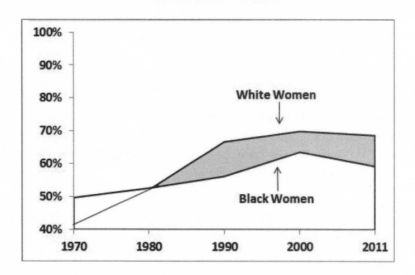

DATA FOR MEN

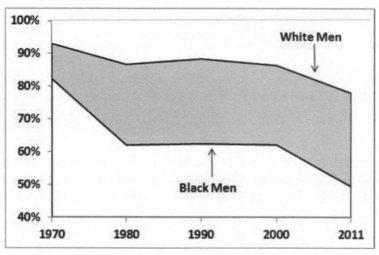

Figure 9.16.   Percent of White and Black Men and Women Age Twenty-Five to Fifty-Nine in Metropolitan Detroit Employed: 1970 to 2011

For white men in the Detroit area, there was a major decline in employment, from 93 percent holding a job in 1970 down to 86 percent in 1990 and then a much greater drop to 78 percent in 2011, reflecting both the long-term trend toward lower rates of labor force participation by men and the national recession that began in 2008. But the decrease among adult white men was modest compared to what happened to black men. By 2011, fewer than one-half of the adult black men in metropolitan Detroit were employed. This is, presumably, a record low employment rate for adult black men in Detroit and in Michigan. In 1940, when Detroit was still greatly impacted by the Depression, 82 percent of the black men in this age group were employed. The industrial restructuring that began in the 1970s is linked to very substantial decreases in the labor force participation and employment of men, especially black men.

Traditionally, the percent of adult women holding a job was higher for blacks than for whites, attributable, in part, to the low wages of black men. As Figure 9.16 shows, a higher proportion of black than white women in metropolitan Detroit were employed in 1970. Employment of women generally increased at least until the 2008 recession began, but in Detroit, as in most other areas, white women entered the labor force more rapidly than black, and so adult white women now are considerably more likely to be employed than black women.

Decreases in employment of adult blacks in metropolitan Detroit help to explain why racial gaps in earnings are getting larger. Figure 9.17 again considers white and black men and women in metropolitan Detroit at ages twenty-five to fifty-nine from 1970 to 2011. This shows per capita earnings in constant 2011 dollars. The trends in what adults earn are influenced both by changes over time in wage rates and changes in employment.

In 1970, adult black men in Detroit earned, on a per capita basis, 62 percent as much as white men. The earnings of white men generally rose until the first decade of this new century, but those of black men fell—moderately at first but quite rapidly in recent years. In terms of their purchasing power, the earnings of adult black men in metropolitan Detroit in 2011 were less than one-half those of similar black men in 1970. And black men in 2011 had per capita earnings only 41 percent those of similarly aged white men—a substantial regression from their relative status in 1970 when they earned 62 percent as much as white men. Compared to white men, black men are much less well off now than in the past in terms of employment and earnings.

Because of their higher employment rates and longer job tenures, black women in metropolitan Detroit in 1970 had higher average earnings than white women, an advantage that persisted into the 1990s. That advantage was lost as white women entered the labor force in much larger numbers

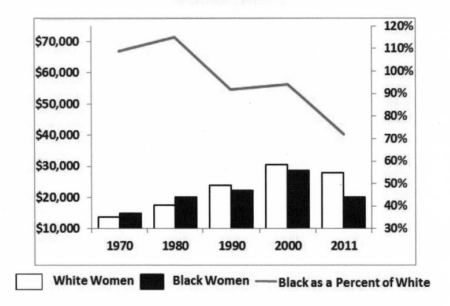

DATA FOR WOMEN

White Women   Black Women   ——Black as a Percent of White

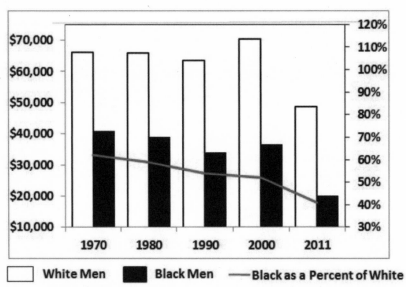

DATA FOR MEN

White Men   Black Men   ——Black as a Percent of White

Figure 9.17.   Per Capita Earnings of White and Black Men and Women Ages Twenty-Five to Fifty-Nine in Metropolitan Detroit 1970 to 2011 (Constant 2011 dollars)

and moved, increasingly, into the high-skilled and high-paying occupations thanks to their investments in higher education. Since the early 2000s earnings in metropolitan Detroit have fallen sharply for most demographic groups, but the drop was especially sharp for black women. By 2011, on a per capita basis they had earnings only 72 percent those of white women.

For most households, earnings are the major source of income. Because of declines in employment among blacks and the drops in their earnings both in absolute terms and relative to whites, it is no surprise that, on average, black households are falling further behind white households in economic status. Figure 9.18 reports the median income of white and black households in metropolitan Detroit from 1970 to 2011 in constant 2011 dollars and reveals the bleak recent trends along with a growing racial gap.

In 1970, there was a substantial racial gap in the purchasing power of households. Black households had median incomes of about 70 percent of those of white households. There was a racial gap of $21,000 in what they could consume in a year. Median incomes for white households reached a peak in 2000 and then plummeted—by 24 percent—in the interval since 2000. Black median household income stagnated before 2000 and then plummeted—by 37 percent—in the years since 2000. As a result, black median household income in 2011 was only one-half that of white households and the actual racial gap in purchasing power had increased to $27,000 in 2011. On

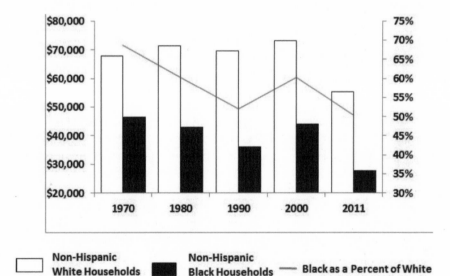

Figure 9.18. Median Income of White and Black Households in Metropolitan Detroit: 1970 to 2011 (Constant 2011 dollars)

economic indicators, African Americans in metropolitan Detroit are falling
further and further behind whites.

How is it possible that the civil rights revolution could produce a social
integration of the races in metropolitan Detroit but a great deterioration of the
economic status of blacks relative to that of whites? A norm of racial diversity has become popular. Major employers are expected to have something
other than white men working in their most public and well-remunerated
jobs. Has this norm of diversity no consequences for African Americans in
metropolitan Detroit? To be sure, there has been a slow emergence of a black
economic elite and, among both races, part of the story is increasing economic
inequality. Those toward the top of the income distribution have fared well in
recent decades while those in the lower half have not. In 1980, a household
in the ninetieth percentile of the white household income distribution had an
income 8.2 times that of a household in the tenth percentile; the distribution
in 2011: 10 times as much. Among black households, the comparable figures
were 13.0 times as much and 14.3. Increasing income inequality means that
those at the top of the distribution can prosper while those toward the middle
and below see their incomes drop.

The reasons why blacks are falling further behind whites on economic
indicators are racial differences in the jobs that blacks and whites held in the
past and racial differences investments in educational attainment. African
Americans, especially black men, were concentrated in the occupations and
industries that substantially downsized their employment due to automa-
tion. In 1970, 47 percent of all employed black men in metropolitan Detroit
worked in durable goods manufacturing—primarily the vehicle industry. The
restructuring of employment in Detroit and the Rust Belt had a much greater
negative impact upon black men than white men.

And then there is the issue of educational attainment. Blacks in the past
have lagged behind whites on most educational indicators and continue to do
so. Figure 9.19 considers the age group that recently completed their investments in education, those aged twenty-five to thirty-four years, and shows the
percent of white and black men and women in metropolitan Detroit reporting
a four-year college degree.

Each date shown in Figure 9.19 represents the college attainment of a
ten-year birth cohort. Not unexpectedly, there is evidence of a trend toward
greater attainment for each of the four groups. For example, the percent of
young white men in metropolitan Detroit with college degrees rose from 22
percent in 1970 to 30 percent at present. However, racial gaps have hardly
closed and, at a time when many of the higher-paying occupations require
college credentials, blacks in metropolitan Detroit lag very far behind
whites in college degrees. The percent of young black men with four-year

DATA FOR WOMEN

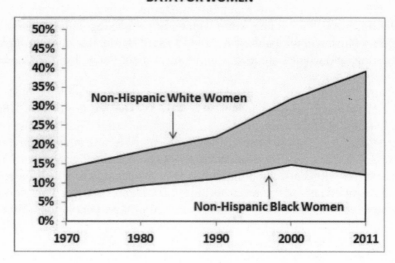

DATA FOR MEN

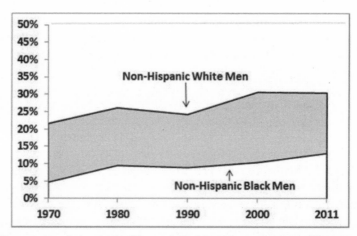

Figure 9.19.   Percent of White and Black Residents of Metropolitan Detroit Ages Twenty-Five to Thirty-Four Reporting a Four-Year College Degree: 1970 to 2011

degrees—13 percent in 2011—was very nearly what it was for white men in 1950. And in both relative and absolute terms, young black women have fallen further behind young white women in completing college. This figure also illustrates the nationwide trend toward the feminization of higher education, and women are increasingly much more likely than men to earn a four-year degree.

Detroit is the only Michigan municipality whose state-appointed financial manager sought Chapter 9 federal bankruptcy protection. However, seven other Michigan cities in recent years have faced such severe financial crises that the state suspended local government and appointed emergency managers to administer all municipal functions. Six of the seven cities with a state-appointed financial manager were either majority African American—Benton Harbor, Flint, Highland Park, and Pontiac—as enumerated in Census 2010 or have substantial black populations: Ecorse and Hamtramck. Two Michigan school districts were eliminated by the state government in the summer of 2013 because of their insolvency: Inkster and Buena Vista. Blacks comprised a substantial percentage of the residents in both districts.

The inability of these cities and school districts to pay their bills is linked to the rapidly declining economic status of Michigan's African American population. Lower incomes are linked to declining property values, less consumer spending, few retail stores, and much lower tax revenues. Municipalities and school districts whose tax base includes largely African American residents have seen their tax revenues shrink in the post–civil rights era. If the black population in Michigan had fared at least as well as whites economically in the last few decades, perhaps the state would have appointed fewer financial managers. To be sure, in metropolitan Detroit suburbanization of middle- and upper-class African Americans also played an important role. In 1980, the suburban black population was only 17 percent as large as the city's and those blacks in the suburbs had per capita incomes 12 percent greater than blacks in the city.

The suburban ring is now open to African Americans. The city of Detroit and its school system—also taken over by the State of Michigan—face great challenges providing the services that its residents expect, so the largest demographic movement at present in the state is the migration of Detroit blacks to the suburbs. In 2011, the suburban black population was 69 percent as large as the city's, and their per capita income was 44 percent greater than that of blacks in the city. City-suburban discrepancies in racial composition may be diminishing but city-suburban differences in economic status are increasing, further exacerbating the city's financial deficiencies.

The Industrial Base

The third major reason explaining the unique conditions found in Detroit is its industrial composition. Municipalities and metropolises grow or decline largely in response to their economic base. If the leading employers expand their output and hire more workers, people will migrate to the location. If you were to ask people about the major reason for the decline of the city of Detroit, many would hasten to point out its reliance upon the vehicle industry. Some would contend that, in the post–World War II years, strong unions demanded pay and fringe benefits that were out of line and, in the long run, unsustainable.

Hence, the auto industry began shifting jobs away from Detroit in the 1950s, a process that accelerated in subsequent decades. Others would blame the management of the vehicle producers contending that at first they foolishly agreed to pay excessively high wages because they could easily raise the price of their vehicles since they faced little competition. Later, managements failed to recognize that European and Asian firms were selling higher-quality but lower-priced cars than those designed and built in Detroit so they quickly lost market share and, eventually, General Motors and Chrysler went bankrupt. Either way, it is easy to blame the decline of the city upon the auto industry.

Detroit truly is the Motor City with its past prosperity and current challenges linked to auto production. If Henry Ford had grown up near Chicago or Cleveland instead of in Dearborn, if Henry Leland had migrated to Milwaukee rather than Detroit, if the Dodge Brothers had moved from Windsor to Toronto instead of to Detroit and if Will Durant, Alfred Sloan, and Walter Chrysler had devoted their entrepreneurial skills to the steel industry or railroading rather than vehicles, Detroit might now be an aging middle-sized industrial city comparable to Akron, Dayton, or Toledo. But, for a variety of reasons including the talents of the aforementioned gentlemen, Detroit became *axes mundi* for vehicle design and production. That industry boomed in the 1920s and workingmen's homes were built throughout the city close to the large and small plants that turned out parts and the cars themselves. Those were not high-style homes when constructed and have not weathered well; indeed, in recent decades many of them have been abandoned. And then, after World War II, the building boom in the city led to the construction of many small bungalows. But, by today's standards, those were tiny homes with miniscule rooms located on small plots. They are probably not the kinds of residences that will appeal to the modest number of young people moving now to Detroit to work in the medical sector or the creative fields. The stock of housing in Detroit is a consequence of the way in which the city's growth was linked to the vehicle industry.

Auto factories and parts plants typically have a limited life span, perhaps five or six decades. When firms go out of business or move their production to the suburban ring, to the American South, or abroad, they often leave behind their antiquated factories. If you drive the streets of Detroit you realize that there are very many small to gigantic vehicle and parts factories that are no longer in use. I do not think that anyone has taken a census of these hundreds of buildings. Some have been very successfully repurposed: Henry Ford's Piquette Street plant now serves as a museum honoring his accomplishments and the Murray Body plant in the Milwaukee Junction area of Detroit has become the Russell Industrial Center, providing office space and ateliers for craftspersons and artists. Those are, perhaps, the exceptions. The nation's iconic industrial ruin is the former Packard Plant with its 2.4 million square feet of floor space now decaying on East Grand Boulevard. And Henry Ford's massive Highland Park plant that once turned out nine thousand Model Ts every workday may soon rival the abandoned Packard Plant. So one important way in which the auto industry had adversely affected the city is its abandonment of numerous buildings throughout the city. Those buildings were erected and operated for decades before environmental concerns became important, so a great deal of remediation may be needed before the structures and the land where they stand might be reused.

To be sure, unions may have won a Pyrrhic victory when managements signed the Treaty of Detroit in 1950 creating a very prosperous blue-collar middle class. But there is a larger issue—that is, increased labor productivity especially in the manufacturing industries and those industries linked to manufacturing. Throughout the nation's industrial history, employers sought to reduce labor costs. Indeed, Henry Ford's perfection of the production line in his Highland Park plant in 1914 greatly lowered labor costs and allowed him to keep cutting the price of the Model T. While there was a long-run trend toward increasing labor productivity by substituting machines for manual labor, the pace apparently accelerated after the early 1970s.

Leaders of the auto industry knew that they faced great competition from foreign producers. They had to drastically increase the quality of their vehicles and simultaneously reduce labor costs. This led to an emphasis upon automating tasks. And then it became feasible to incorporate the computer and information technology to enhance quality. Economic censuses are conducted on a five-year schedule. Between 1972 and 2007, they report that the number of workers employed by manufacturing firms within the city of Detroit fell by 80 percent. Linked to that trend, the number of retail trade establishments in the city declined by 78 percent in the same interval.

As an illustration of what has occurred recently with labor productivity, consider information presented in figure 9.20. These data, calculated by the

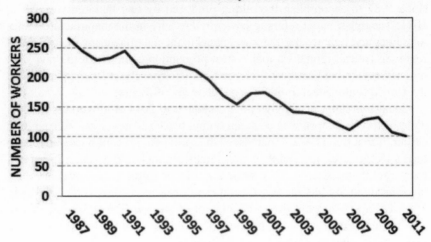

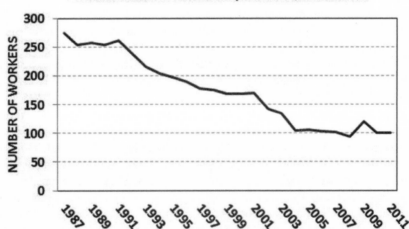

Figure 9.20.   Indexes of Labor Productivity in the Vehicle and Steel Industries: 1987 to 2011

federal Bureau of Labor Statistics refer to the manufacture of cars and light trucks. The figures show how many workers would be needed in each year since 1987 to accomplish the output produced by one hundred workers in 2011. The upper panel refers to labor productivity in the manufacture of automobiles and light trucks; the lower panel to the manufacturing of steel. Metropolitan Detroit remains a major steel production center with the raw steel mill of Severstal in Dearborn—Henry Ford's former River Rouge plant—and the United States Steel mills on Zug Island and in Ecorse.

Changes in labor productivity are dramatic. In 2011, 100 workers in a vehicle factory could produce as much output as 265 workers just a generation earlier. If that trend toward increased labor productivity continues into the future, a Detroit area auto plant six years in the future could produce 25 percent more cars than today with the same sized labor force. In the steel industry, labor productivity has increased even more, since, in 2011, it required only 100 workers to turn out the same amount of steel as 274 employees did in 1987. Improvements in labor productivity are similar in the railroad industry and in most other manufacturing industries.

When we compare Detroit to the other metropolises that include the nation's largest cities, we can see how improvements in labor productivity have had an especially great impact here. Figure 9.21 considers the metropolitan areas that include the nation's twenty-five largest cities in 2012 and shows the percentage of their employed workers holding jobs in durable goods manufacturing industries or on railroads in 1970. Railroads are included since most durable goods firms get their inputs and ship their products by rail. The year 1970 was selected since it was just before the oil embargo that appears to be a turning point for vehicle producers and their suppliers.

Detroit was distinctive, among the nation's largest metropolises in 1970 for the concentration of its employment in durable goods manufacturing. About one-third of all Detroit area workers were in those industries. Data are not shown here but the percent in durable goods manufacturing was much higher in Detroit in 1970 than in other well-known Rust Belt metropolises including Buffalo, Cleveland, and Pittsburgh. It is not so much that auto production has disappeared in Detroit and in Michigan. It has not. Since 1970, three new production plants have opened in the city of Detroit—Jefferson North, Hamtramck Assembly, and Conner Avenue—and those in the suburban ring have been modernized.

However, a rather small number of workers in these plants now turn out what would have required four or more times as many workers in 1970. Metropolitan San Jose was second to Detroit in proportion of workers in durable goods manufacturing in 1970. Industrial and mechanical engineers have learned how to increase productivity with regard to the auto industry but much less so for the design of computers and the drafting of software.

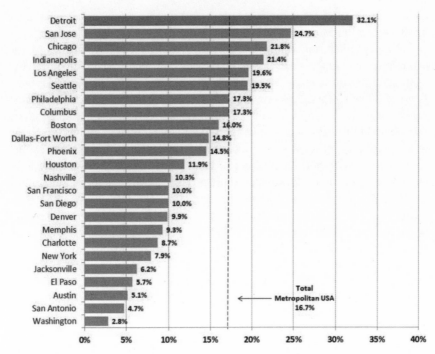

Figure 9.21. Percent of Employed Persons Working in Durable Goods Manufacturing and for Railroads: 1970 for Metropolitan Areas Containing the Nation's Twenty-Five Largest Cities in 2010

Because of the age of the plants in the city, Detroit has been much more impacted by increases in labor productivity and other changes than the suburban ring. To be sure, large numbers of manufacturing jobs have disappeared in the metropolis, but the loss has, apparently, been sharper in the city. The Census Bureau employment estimates suggest that in the first decade of this century, the number of manufacturing jobs in the Detroit suburban ring declined by 36 percent; within the city by 47 percent.

One might think that civic leaders in Detroit and Michigan would have recognized how the state's employment structure was changing rapidly and would have taken steps to diversify the economic base. Perhaps if unions had been thwarted and a system of tax breaks had been put into place, the number of jobs in metropolitan Detroit would have risen. I think that is unrealistic. In the absence of high wages and strong unions, it is possible that Detroit could have become a center for low-wage, low-skill manufacturing, but it is likely that much lower wages in Asia would have driven Detroit firms out of business. If we consider metropolises that have grown rapidly, we find that they have been favored by macro-economic and demographic trends that were hardly subject to the control of city officials or state governors.

Since manufacturing employment peaked, the most rapidly growing large economic sectors have been financial services, the health sector, advanced education, and professional services including the law. Detroit has employment in all of those sectors, but certainly not as much as many other cities. Boston was a stagnant metropolis into the 1950s, but innovative individuals there contributed to the development of computer technology and, in the 1960s, the federal government substantially increased their funding for higher education, scientific research, and medical costs. Institutions in and near that city were able to capitalize upon those opportunities. New York City faced bankruptcy in the 1960s and the state supervised its spending. But that city was favorably positioned to both capitalize upon the great increase in financial services employment and benefit from the liberalization of immigration laws that occurred after Michigan senator Phil Hart sponsored a reform in 1965.

Cities in the South and the West benefited from low energy costs and both internal migration—the long-run trend of people moving from cold to warmer climates—and international immigration. And Washington, D.C., has come to rival San Francisco as the most prosperous city in the country because of changes in our federal government, namely the tremendous increase in the number of lawyers, consultants, advocates, and other experts with advanced educations who find well-paid employment representing organizations and interests in the nation's capital. Much of the time while these other locations were growing, the Detroit metropolitan area was riven by a city-suburban divide that, in the past but not so much at present, was also a black-white divide. And the largest employers in the metropolitan Detroit area were struggling to compete with each other and with foreign producers, a process that strongly encouraged drastic reductions in employment. As a result, Detroit fell behind many other metropolises in economic status and population size, culminating in the city's seeking bankruptcy protection from federal court.

DETROIT: WHAT IS GOING TO
HAPPEN IN THE NEXT TWENTY-FIVE YEARS?

Kurt Metzger, director of the Data Driven Detroit organization, has described contemporary Detroit as a tale of two cities. He means that there are some very favorable developments implying a bright future for at least some sections of the city. At the same time, there are many problems of poverty, lack of human capital, and decay of neighborhoods that are hardly being addressed at present.

To start with the positive, major capital investments have been made in manufacturing facilities in Detroit and the suburban ring. The metropolis will continue to be a center for the design and production of vehicles. After several billion dollars of investments by Chrysler, Daimler, and now Fiat, the Jefferson North plant in Detroit, by 2013, was producing thirty thousand Jeep Cherokees and Dodge Durangos each month, with a retail sales price approximating $900 million. The once underutilized General Motors Hamtramck Assembly plant—located in Detroit and Hamtramck—now assembles Volts, Malibus, Impalas, and Amporas. Just beyond the city's limits, the recently modernized Ford River Rouge is the assembly site where about twenty-five thousand Ford F-150s are built each month—the nation's most popular vehicle.

Ford assembly plants in suburban Wayne and Flat Rock have recently been modernized at substantial costs. The new Focus is now built in Wayne and the new Fusion in Flat Rock. Chrysler-Fiat, in 2013, announced major multimillion-dollar investments in three area plants—one in Detroit—to turn out more modern and fuel-efficient engines. The share of North American vehicle production occurring in the Detroit area may now be increasing after years of decline. And major investments have been made by other industries linked to the auto industry. Severstal recently completed a modernization costing more than $500 million. Marathon Oil, located in southwest Detroit, in 2012 finished a $2.1 billion renovation of their facility so as to efficiently refine Alberta tar sands into petroleum. Detroit will continue to be a major manufacturing center, although output is likely to increase much more rapidly than employment. For example, the Marathon Oil huge investment created fewer than one hundred fifty new jobs. Detroit is certainly not going to disappear as a major manufacturing center. The output of the area's manufacturing firms seems likely to increase, but employment gains may be modest because of the continuing trend toward much greater labor productivity.

Downtown and midtown Detroit are among the prosperous and expanding areas of the city. More than a decade ago, three casinos opened in or near downtown Detroit. And then major new parks were built in downtown for the Detroit Tigers and Detroit Lions. This provoked the opening of a wide array of new restaurants and night clubs and the renovation of long-shuttered hotels: The Book Cadillac; the Fort Shelby; and, more recently, the Pontchartrain. Downtown redevelopment accelerated when General Motors acquired the Renaissance Center and moved their offices there. Later, Compuware and Blue Cross-Blue Shield shifted substantial numbers of employees from the suburban ring to downtown and joined in a targeted and now popular program to provide financial incentives for their workers who wished to rent an apartment or buy a condo near center city.

Recently, Dan Gilbert of Quicken Loans has, through his real estate firm, purchased or taken options on more than two dozen office buildings in downtown Detroit. Presumably, he is interested in attracting information technology specialists. Future innovations in vehicles are likely to depend upon creative designers who will produce the software and hardware that will make vehicles much safer and more efficient because they will tell us about our driving; warn us of dangers ahead; and, eventually, possibly make our vehicles into smart cars that will drive themselves. Will the imaginative work needed for smart cars be accomplished in Silicon Valley or in architecturally significant buildings in downtown Detroit? If Dan Gilbert's efforts make downtown Detroit a center for such talented individuals—and the many lawyers, professional engineers, and consultants who will be involved—Detroit may develop a dynamic center city with a large professional labor force.

Midtown Detroit is also an area of growth. Detroit Medical Center and Henry Ford Hospital are major medical campuses and Wayne State's Medical School is the largest in the nation. Three years ago, when the Vanguard Health system purchased Detroit Medical Center, they promised to invest $900 million in new facilities. Within two weeks after that announcement, Henry Ford Hospital announced that they would invest $500 million in new facilities within the next decade. They are now erecting a new campus on West Grand Boulevard in Detroit's New Center area. These investments are driven, in part, by the rapid aging of the population. The number of Michigan residents age sixty-five and over in 2030 will be about 50 percent larger than at present. Medical-sector employment is likely to soon equal durable goods manufacturing employment in metropolitan Detroit. In 2011, two hundred thirty-one thousand Detroit-area residents were working in the medical sector; two hundred seventy-three thousand in manufacturing. Wayne State University continues to expand, contributing to a population increase and economic development. After the College for Creative Studies received a $50 million gift from the estate of Josephine Ford, they established a new campus in General Motors' Argonaut Building. Downtown Detroit and midtown appear to be locations of continuing increases in employment and may be welcoming growing numbers of young professionals and creative artists who find attractive opportunities there. Perhaps less frequently cited is the development of residential and commercial activities in a corridor along Detroit's riverfront from the Renaissance Center north to the border with Grosse Pointe Park.

There are, however, many other sections of the city. To be sure, there are two dozen or so attractive neighborhoods with appealing residences. The homes in some neighborhoods have architectural appeal, such as the Victorian and Queen Anne residences in the Woodbridge neighborhoods, the East

Ferry Street Historic District, and the West Canfield Historic District. Other neighborhoods have a more modest stock of homes but have an eclectic appeal such as Corktown. And there are Detroit neighborhoods where the entrepreneurs of the early auto era invested their savings in elegant, spacious architect-designed homes that maintain their charm, including Indian Village, Palmer Woods, Sherwood Forest, Barry Subdivision, and the University District. Those neighborhoods, however, are exceptions. In vast stretches of Detroit modest workingmen's homes were built and many of them have lost whatever appeal they had.

We do not know what will happen to Detroit's request for federal court bankruptcy. Perhaps, in the best circumstances, the federal court will allow bankruptcy and the judge will act quickly. It is possible that, within a couple of years, the city will emerge from the litigation freed from the obligation to pay many of its current debts. If so, will a new mayor and elected city government officials be able to address the issues of providing excellent city services so competent that city residents might be reluctant to leave for the suburbs? Will the residents and commercial activities in a prospering downtown, midtown and riverfront along with those industrial locations that pay substantial property taxes including the vehicle assembly plants be able to support the city? I think that you need to be an optimist to give an affirmative answer to that question.

Detroit is a very large city. One of the more frequently republished maps shows that Manhattan, Boston, and San Francisco could fit inside the city limits of Detroit. The city needs to provide police, fire, and emergency medical services for all of that area. Extensive stretches of the city have housing units of marginal value, places where the population seems destined to continue decreasing. If it were easy to downsize cities, there would be good examples of how that might be accomplished. Frankly, there are few such examples. Michigan laws make it almost impossible for a city to evict people from their homes, even if there are just a few occupied residences on a block. And, there is little demand for land in Detroit. Will the city, after bankruptcy, have the resources to encourage current residents to remain in and new residents to enter the current middle-class and attractive neighborhoods? Will there be resources to bolster the future of other neighborhoods that are on the cusp of sliding into decline? A realistic view is that there will be many Detroit buildings and neighborhoods for future ruin porn photographers.

Many of the fundamental challenges remain and will not be addressed by an emergency manager or federal bankruptcy court. There is the Detroit metropolitan area issue of fostering economic development and employment growth. Throughout the metropolis, there are the educational challenges involving the closing of many elementary and secondary schools in response to population decline and low fertility while steadily increasing achievement of the students who remain. And then there is the metropolitan-wide challenge of improving postsecondary schools so that students are well prepared for jobs and careers that are available. There are metropolitan challenges regarding environment concerns, public transportation, and a parks system that will capitalize upon the area's many attractive features. Will there be the gradual emergence of effective metropolitan solutions? Or will metropolitan Detroit continue to by a location with one large but financially troubled city surrounded by more than one hundred suburbs and almost as many suburban school districts, each competing for resources, some with success but with quite a few others eventually facing the fiscal crisis that characterized Detroit in 2013?

What is needed is "a change of the basis of society" (Ellison 1995, 340). If we fail in this task (the task of fundamentally reimagining America), Ellison argued, a study like Myrdal's could be "used for less democratic purposes." We now know this to be true, and what is most startling is that even the aspirational claims of Dr. King have been used for less democratic purposes. In so many ways, he and the movement out of which he comes have "become an instrument of an American tragedy," as Ellison put it, that keeps us sleepwalking. Telling a different story is the beginning of waking up.

BIBLIOGRAPHY

Binelli, Mark. 2012. *Detroit City Is the Place to Be.* New York: Henry Holt and Company.
Ellison, Ralph, 1995. "*An American Dilemma*: A Review." In *The Collected Essays of Ralph Ellison.* New York: Modern Library.
Gallagher, John. 2013. *Revolution Detroit: Strategies for Urban Reinvention.* Detroit: Wayne State University Press.
Glaeser, Edward. 2011. *Triumph of the City: How Our Greatest Invention Makes Us Richer, Smarter, Greener, Healthier, and Happier.* New York: Penguin Press.
Massey, Douglas S., and Nancy A. Denton. 1993. *American Apartheid: Segregation and the Making of the Underclass.* Cambridge: Harvard University Press.
Moore, Andrew. 2010. *Detroit Disassembled.* Akron, Ohio: Akron Art Museum.
Sugrue, Thomas J. 1996. *The Origins of the Urban Crisis: Race and Inequality in Postwar Detroit.* Princeton, NJ: Princeton University Press.
Taubman, Julia Reyes. 2012. *Detroit: 138 Square Miles.* Detroit: Museum of Contemporary Art.
Vergara, Camilo José. 1995. *The New American Ghetto.* New Brunswick, NJ: Rutgers University Press.

Chapter Ten

Racial Disparities in Economic Well-Being in the Detroit Metropolitan Area after the Great Recession

Lucie Kalousova and Sheldon Danziger

African Americans are more disadvantaged in the labor market compared to non-Hispanic whites across all phases of the business cycle (Freeman 1973). Their disadvantage widens during recessionary periods because black and low-skilled workers are often the first to lose their jobs when the economy slows (Brown and Pagán 1998, Couch and Fairlie 2010, Freeman 1973). The Great Recession, which officially lasted from December 2007 to June 2009, confirmed this long-standing labor market pattern. While the national unemployment rate for whites peaked around 8.7 percent in June 2009, the rate for blacks reached 15 percent in April and May 2009. Many have thus suggested that economic disparities between black and white Americans will grow as a result of the recession and the ensuing slow recovery. In this chapter, we focus on how black and white residents of the three-county Detroit metropolitan area (Wayne, Oakland, and Macomb counties) were faring in the aftermath of the Great Recession. We examine racial disparities in three domains of economic well-being: employment, housing, and financial security.

Although the unemployment rate is an important indicator of economic hardship in the population, the severity of the Great Recession was compounded by the collapse in stock prices, beginning in mid-2008, and in housing prices, that began in 2006. As housing values dropped precipitously, interest rates of adjustable mortgages rose, forcing many homeowners to default on their payments. Most vulnerable to the resulting "foreclosure epidemic" were borrowers with adjustable subprime mortgages, a recent banking product offered to those judged to pose a greater-than-average credit risk to lenders.

Among blacks and whites with comparable credit scores, blacks were more likely to be offered a subprime rather than conventional mortgage (Bond and

Williams 2007). Moreover, blacks living in predominantly black communities had higher risk of foreclosure after falling behind or defaulting on their mortgages than were blacks and whites who lived in predominantly white areas (Rugh and Massey 2010). In the Detroit metropolitan area, 29 percent of new mortgages that were approved in 2005 were considered subprime, the fifth-highest rate of subprime lending in the country (Mayer and Pence 2008). African American residents of this highly racially segregated city were therefore at high risk for housing instability when the housing market collapsed.

For many Americans, the Great Recession caused substantial losses in wealth, both due to the housing crisis and the stock market collapse. Pfeffer, Danziger, and Schoeni (2013) report that between 2007 and 2011, about one-fourth of American households lost at least 75 percent of their net worth and half lost at least 25 percent. Because blacks have a larger proportion of their wealth comprised of housing assets relative to whites, their losses were disproportionately greater (Shapiro, Meschede, and Osoro 2013). Between 2005 and 2009, the median wealth of an African American household fell by 53 percent compared to 16 percent for whites. The large pre-recession racial disparity in net worth thus widened after the recession—in 2004, white median household wealth was eleven times greater than that of black households, but by 2009, this ratio rose to nineteen (Kochhar, Taylor, and Fry 2011).

The Great Recession officially ended in June 2009, but the economic recovery has been slow, with the national unemployment rate in July 2014 at 6.2 percent. The unemployment rate remains higher and the labor force participation lower than they were prior to the start of the recession. Assuming the pace of current employment gains continues, it will take four or five years to approach the employment and labor force participation rate of 2007 (Burtless 2013). For Detroit, with much higher unemployment, it could take another decade. Monitoring changes in household well-being as the economy recovers is a key goal of the Michigan Recession and Recovery Study (MRRS), a survey developed and administered by the National Poverty Center at the University of Michigan. Using these data, we evaluate how black and white Detroiters have fared in terms of financial insecurity, housing instability, poverty, and net worth, with a focus on change in disparities, in the aftermath of the Great Recession through mid-2011.

DATA AND MEASURES

MRRS data were collected in face-to-face interviews, about one hour in length, with a stratified random sample of English-speaking non-institutionalized adults between the ages of nineteen and sixty-four who lived in Macomb, Oakland, and Wayne counties in fall 2009, shortly after the official end of the Great Recession.[1] The baseline survey was fielded from October 2009 to April 2010, and the second wave of interviews was conducted from April to August of 2011. MRRS was designed with an oversample of African Americans and includes mainly African American and non-Hispanic white respondents, reflecting the Detroit area's residential composition.

At the first wave, 914 respondents completed interviews, with a response rate of 82.8 percent. At the second wave, 847 of the surviving wave one respondents were re-interviewed with a response rate of 93.9 percent. Survey weights calculated for each survey wave address nonresponse and make the MRRS representative of working-age adults living in the three-county area. MRRS contains information about multiple domains of the respondents' lives, such as income, wealth, employment histories, health and health care access, family composition, and social support. It also includes extensive information about recent hardships they may have experienced that we use to construct indicators of economic hardships. More detailed information about the survey can be found in Kalousova and Burgard (2013).

Financial Insecurity. We classified respondents as financially insecure if they reported any of these five adverse events: filing for bankruptcy, being behind on rent or mortgage, taking a payday loan or cash advance, having a credit card cancelled involuntarily, and falling behind on paying utilities. The questions were asked in reference to the past twelve months, except for those on being behind on rent or mortgage, which were asked in reference to "now," that is, at the time of the interview. We combined responses to two questions, "Are you currently behind on rent?" for renters and "Are you paying off this loan [mortgage] ahead of schedule, behind schedule, or are you payments about on schedule?" for mortgage holders.

Housing Instability. Respondents are classified as having experienced housing instability if they reported having moved for cost reasons; had experienced homelessness, eviction, or foreclosure; and/or had moved in with someone else to share expenses. Each experience was reported for the twelve months prior to the interview. We combined the questions on evictions and foreclosures in the past twelve months in order to have a comparable measure for renters and homeowners.

Poverty. We measured poverty by constructing an income-to-needs ratio based on reported household income plus food stamps in the previous calendar year, household composition, and the federal poverty threshold. For calendar year 2010, the poverty line for a family of four persons was $22,050 (Federal Register 2010).

Zero or Negative Net Worth. Net worth is defined as total assets less total debts. We created a binary indicator of whether respondents had zero or negative net worth.

Other Relevant Variables. Respondents were asked, "What race are you?" We designated respondents who self-identified as African American as black (23 percent). Due to a small number of Hispanics and Asians in the sample, we included their responses with those of whites. In the multivariate analyses, we also accounted for age of the respondent, gender, educational attainment (more than a high school diploma versus high school diploma or less), and self-rated health.

ANALYTIC STRATEGY

In order to compare the differences in the experience of economic hardships in the aftermath of the recession for black and white respondents, we employed logistic regression models predicting the likelihood of each hardship at each wave for black and white males with no more education than a high school diploma only in good health and who were between the ages of thirty-five and fifty at the first wave. We tested the statistical significance of the differences between blacks and whites at the first wave and then at the second wave. We also tested the significance of the difference in the prevalence of each hardship reported by blacks at the first wave and the same respondents at the second, and the significance of the difference in the prevalence of each hardship reported by whites at the first time point and the same respondents at the second. Finally, we tested the significance of the differences in the rate of change in the prevalence of each hardship between the two groups.

RESULTS

Table 10.1 displays demographic characteristics of the total sample (weighted) and divided by race. We find no statistical differences in the mean age and gender of black and white respondents. However, whites were significantly more likely to be married (65 versus 31 percent) and less likely to have no education beyond a high school diploma (58 percent versus 69). Whites also report better health (3.71 versus 3.13) and higher mean household income ($87,164 versus $35,580).

In figure 10.1, we display the unemployment rate and labor force nonparticipation rate of the MRRS respondents between January 2007 and March 2011, as collected by the retrospective employment status calendar adminis-

Table 10.1. Sociodemographic characteristics and hardship experiences of Michigan Recession and Recovery Study respondents by race at baseline, presented as means and their standard deviations or percentages.

	Overall	Black	SD	Non-black	SD
Age in years (mean)	42.41	41.10	19.62	42.79	10.04
% Married	57%	31%	—	65%	—
% Female	51%	55%	—	50%	—
% HS diploma or less	60%	69%	—	58%	—
Self-Rated Health (mean; 1 = poor; 5 = excellent)	3.58	3.13	1.82	3.71	0.82
Household Income in 2009 (mean)	75,516	35,580	53,000	87,164	65,255
N	847	404		442	

Note: *p<.05, **p<.01, ***p<.001. Figures are all weighted.

tered at both survey waves. From spring 2007 through September of 2008, the monthly unemployment rate for whites ranged between 5 and 9 percent. In the later part of 2008, it rose above 10 percent, where it mostly remained through March 2011. The percentage of whites out of the labor force ranged from a high of around 18 percent in spring 2007 to a low of 13 percent in spring 2008, later rising above 15 percent again.

Both the unemployment rate and the labor force nonparticipation rate fluctuated much more for blacks compared to whites. The unemployment rate of blacks was extraordinarily high prior to the recession, about 20 percent in fall 2007, and rose markedly in spring 2008, reaching almost 30 percent for most of 2009. It began declining in the winter of 2009/2010, but remained near 22 percent from winter 2010 until spring 2011. The percentage of blacks out of the labor force increased steadily from 17 percent in January 2007 to 21 percent in September 2009 before reaching about 30 percent in early 2010. This

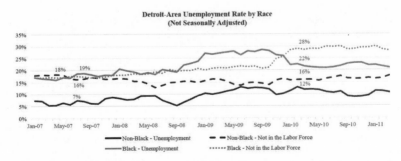

Figure 10.1. Unemployment rate and labor force non-participation rate of the Michigan Recession and Recovery Study respondents.

increased labor force nonparticipation coincided with a decrease in the black unemployment rate of a similar magnitude, suggesting that some of the recent decline in unemployment in the Detroit area can be attributed to discouraged workers who stopped looking for work.

In table 10.2, we display unadjusted (bivariate) distributions of hardships by race at the first and second survey waves. There are statistically significant differences between blacks and whites on all four hardship measures at both waves. While 28 percent of whites experienced financial insecurity at wave 1, 48 percent of blacks did. At wave 2, financial insecurity increased to 52 percent for blacks, but fell slightly to 26 percent for whites. At wave 1, 19 percent of whites and 43 percent blacks experienced housing instability. At wave 2, housing instability fell to 13 percent among whites and to 34 percent among blacks. The poverty rate was 5 percent for whites but 38 percent for blacks at wave 1 and 6 percent for whites and 43 percent for blacks at wave 2. Finally, a quarter of whites and 45 percent of blacks had zero or negative net worth at the first wave; at the second wave, the percentage of whites with zero or negative net worth decreased slightly to 23 percent, but this percentage for blacks increased to 48 percent. In sum, hardships were extensive for both races, but much longer for blacks. And between the two waves, three of the hardship measures decreased slightly for whites, but increased for blacks.

Figure 10.2 shows the predicted probability of financial insecurity for blacks and whites, obtained by constructing logistic regression models, for a male respondent with no more than a high school diploma, in good health, and between the ages of thirty-five and fifty. Similar to the unadjusted results displayed in table 10.2, the difference in the overall probability of financial insecurity between blacks and whites is statistically significant at both waves. Blacks had a .48 probability of experiencing financial insecurity at the first wave and a .53 probability at the second wave. For whites, on the other hand,

Table 10.2. Hardship experiences of Michigan Recession and Recovery Study respondents by race at baseline and follow-up, presented as percentages.

	2009/10			2011		
	Non-Black	*Black*	*p for diff*	*Non-Black*	*Black*	*p for diff*
Financial Insecurity	28%	48%	***	26%	52%	***
Housing Instability	19%	43%	***	13%	34%	***
In Poverty	5%	38%	***	6%	43%	***
Zero or Negative Net-worth	25%	45%	***	23%	48%	***
N		404	442		404	442

Note: *p<.05, **p<.01, ***p<.001. Figures are all weighted.

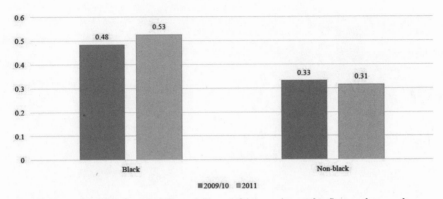

Figure 10.2. **Predicted probability of financial insecurity at the first and second wave of the survey by race.**

we observed a small decline from 0.33 to 0.31. Neither the increase in the probability of financial insecurity for blacks, nor the decrease for whites represented a statistically significant change within each group over time. Moreover, the difference of their differences, that is, the differential rate of change in financial insecurity for blacks (+0.05) and whites (-0.02) between waves, was not statistically significant either, indicating that the two trends had not diverged in a statistically detectable way.

Figure 10.3 exhibits the predicted probability of housing instability obtained analogously to the regression method used for figure 10.2. Again, similar to the unadjusted results from table 10.2, the differences between adjusted predicted probabilities between blacks and whites are statistically significant at both waves. The predicted probability of housing instability decreased from 0.37 to 0.29 for blacks and from 0.18 to 0.12 for whites. This was a statistically significant improvement within each group. The overall difference in the rate of improvement in housing instability between blacks (-0.08) and whites (-0.06) between waves is, however, not significant.

Figure 10.4 shows a very large significant difference between the likelihood of being poor for black and white Detroit residents. The predicted probability for blacks increased from 0.13 to 0.17 between waves, but this was not a statistically significant change. For whites, it increased slightly from 0.01 to 0.02. The difference in the rate of change between the racial groups was also not statistically significant.

In figure 10.5, we present differences in predicted probability of having zero or negative net worth. As is the case for all of the hardships measured, the difference in the predicted probability between blacks and whites was

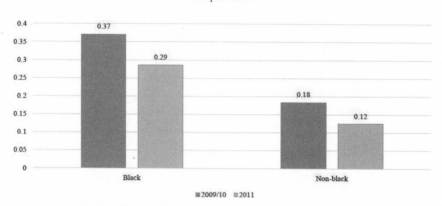

Figure 10.3.   Predicted probability of housing insecurity at the first and second wave of the survey by race.

statistically significant at both waves. The predicted probability of zero or negative net worth increased from 0.47 to 0.51 for blacks and decreased from 0.28 to 0.27 for whites, but neither the within-group increase for blacks nor the within-group decrease for whites was significant, and neither was the difference in the rate of change for blacks (+0.04) and whites (-0.01).

DISCUSSION

Long before the onset of the Great Recession, economic disadvantages were unevenly distributed along racial lines in the Detroit metropolitan area

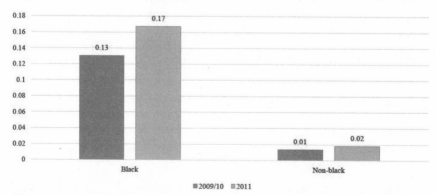

Figure 10.4.   Predicted probability of being in poverty at the first and second wave of the survey by race.

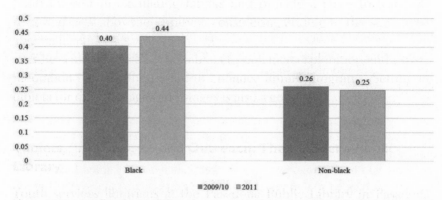

Figure 10.5. Predicted probability of zero or negative net-worth at the first and second wave of the survey by race.

(Farley, Danziger, and Holzer 2000). In addition, some recent national-level studies suggest that the disparities between blacks and whites have grown even wider after the Great Recession (Kochhar, Taylor, and Fry 2011; Pfeffer, Danziger, and Schoeni 2013). The results of our study document stark post-recession disparities between blacks and whites in four domains of hardship, and demonstrate that these large differences remained unchanged or increased between 2009 and 2011.

At the second survey interview, in 2011, many blacks and whites alike were experiencing serious economic difficulties. The extent of three of the four hardships was generally lower at wave 2 than at wave 1 for white Detroiters, whereas black residents saw the prevalence of every hardship, except housing instability, rise slightly. However, these divergent trends were not large enough to achieve statistical significance in a regression framework.

There are several caveats regarding the findings. The lack of statistical significance could be an artifact of the relatively small sample size in MRRS. Future analysis of the third survey wave will allow us to draw conclusions about the divergence or convergence of the economic well-being of the two groups through 2013. Nevertheless, our findings suggest that the prevalence of post-recession hardship has mostly increased for the black population in the three-county area between 2009 and 2011, while it has mostly decreased for whites.

Public Policies to Reduce Disparities

Given the current economic and public policy contexts, unemployment, poverty, and income and wealth disparities by race/ethnicity in the United

States in general and in the Detroit metropolitan area in particular are not likely to fall substantially in the near future. However, these disparities could be reduced if the public and policy makers muster the political will to pursue a range of promising social and economic policies. Here, we emphasize changes in policies designed to raise employment and earnings, and those designed to raise educational attainment.

These policies further two primary goals. The first is "to make work pay." This requires that government regulations about wages and working conditions (such as the minimum wage or the ability of workers to unionize) and government benefits for low-wage workers (such as the Earned Income Tax Credit) be changed so that most full-time workers can avoid poverty. For example, the federal minimum wage has not been increased since 2007, and its 2013 value, when adjusted for inflation, is lower than it was in the late 1960s. Since its introduction in the mid-1970s, the Earned Income Tax Credit has been substantially increased for families with children and now significantly raises the incomes of low-wage workers with children. But it provides minimal assistance for childless single and married workers.

The United States has not had a large public-service employment program since the early 1980s, when President Ronald Reagan terminated the Comprehensive Employment and Training Act (CETA). Because the 1996 welfare reform greatly reduced access to cash assistance, there is a pressing need for public jobs of last resort, especially when the unemployment rate is above 4 percent. These jobs can provide work opportunities for those who are willing to work but cannot find steady employment in regular private or public sector jobs either because of poor economic conditions or because they face substantial employment barriers (e.g., physical health and mental health problems, learning disabilities, etc.) that make it difficult for them to work steadily. Workers in last-resort jobs could perform socially beneficial tasks for which there is little effective labor demand, such as labor-intensive public services in disadvantaged communities—neighborhood maintenance, weatherizing homes, assisting the elderly.

In recent years, the labor market has seen substantial progress in reducing gender disparities, as women's employment and earnings have increased relative to those of men (DiPrete and Buchmann 2013). Although racial and ethnic disparities in employment and earnings have narrowed since the passage of the Civil Rights Act fifty years ago, they remain large and some have even widened. For example, young black men face substantially worse labor market opportunities than similar white non-Hispanic men, a gap that both reflects and contributes to high levels of incarceration (Pettit 2012).

Reducing labor market discrimination, and thereby raising employment rates and earnings among marginalized groups, should become a higher priority for public policy than it has been.

Our second goal was a key focus of the War on Poverty—increased investments in education and training over the life course (Bailey and Danziger 2013). Even though Americans have always favored providing a "hand up" instead of a "hand out" to reduce poverty and promote mobility, federal spending on education and training programs for disadvantaged youth and adults has fallen dramatically since the early 1980s (Holzer 2009).

The nation's education system falls well short of providing low-income students the skills they need to succeed in the twenty-first-century labor market. More effective early childhood and K–12 educational policies would result in fewer high school dropouts, more community college degrees and certificates, and more four-year college degrees. Educational policies remain appealing to the public, but in the short term they are more expensive than policies that make work pay for today's adults. And, the payoffs from successful programs—increased schooling, employment, and earnings and lower rates of incarceration and non-marital births when the children reach adulthood—require many years to materialize. A substantial investment into the nation's public education system is an economically feasible and socially just strategy for reducing disparities in the long run (Duncan and Murnane 2011).

These policies are modest—they do not attempt to stop or reverse the processes of globalization and labor-saving technological change that continue to transform our economy. They accept the fact that the economy generates economic hardship for millions of workers but contend that government policies should do more to cushion those negatively affected by the evolving restructuring of the global economy.

These policies are neither race nor place specific; rather, they seek to raise the employment and incomes of all low-income workers and families. They would, however, disproportionately benefit African Americans and other racial/ethnic groups who have lower-than-average earnings and higher-than-average unemployment and poverty rates, including those who live in areas of concentrated poverty, such as in the city of Detroit.

CONCLUSION

Did the Great Recession exacerbate economic disparities between black and white Detroiters? Most likely, yes. The differences in economic well-being that we have documented remain stark. They did not emerge because of the Great Recession. Rather, they have deep roots in the racial tensions and economic changes of the last four decades of the twentieth century, including suburbanization, globalization, labor-saving technological changes and the resulting precipitous decline of living conditions in the Motor City (Farley,

Danziger, and Holzer 2000). The future well-being of metro-area residents is also clouded by the fact that Detroit's emergency manager, Kevyn Orr, filed for Chapter 9 bankruptcy in July 2013. The popular press welcomed this step with mixed feelings, offering both scenarios of the impending ultimate urban decline as well as prospects of recovery. We view the bankruptcy declaration, and the possible emergence from bankruptcy in 2015, as an opportunity for the city and its people. If, after discharging some of its debts, it directs funds toward improvements in public transportation that will better connect workers to jobs, intensify revitalization efforts, and place greater emphasis on antidiscrimination efforts in public policy, then the bankruptcy could mark a positive turn for reducing the racial economic disparities of Detroit.

NOTE

1. The National Bureau of Economic Research (NBER) Business Cycle Dating Committee decides on the official beginnings of both economic recoveries and expansions. The official end of the recession was June 2009. See: http://www.nber.org/cycles/recessions_faq.html

REFERENCES

Bailey, Martha J., and Sheldon Danziger. 2013. *Legacies of the War on Poverty.* New York: Russell Sage Foundation.

Bond, C., and R. Williams. 2007. "Residential Segregation and the Transformation of Home Mortgage Lending." *Social Forces* 86(2): 671–98.

Brown, C. J., and J. A. Pagán. 1998. "Changes in Employment Status across Demographic Groups during the 1990–1991 Recession." *Applied Economics* 30(12): 1571–83.

Burtless, Gary. 2013. "The Unemployment Rate Is Edging Down, and the Job Picture Slowly Improving." *Hamilton Project*, Washington, DC. Retrieved August 6, 2013, from http://www.brookings.edu/blogs/jobs/posts/2013/08/02-jobs-unemployment-rate-burtless.

Couch, K. A., and R. Fairlie. 2010. "Last Hired, First Fired? Black-White Unemployment and the Business Cycle." *Demography* 47(1): 227–47.

DiPrete, Thomas A., and Claudia Buchmann. 2013. *The Rise of Women: The Growing Gender Gap in Education and What It Means for American Schools.* New York: Russell Sage Foundation.

Duncan, Greg J., and Richard J. Murnane. 2011. *Whither Opportunity? Rising Inequality, Schools, and Children's Life Chances.* New York: Russell Sage Foundation.

Farley, Reynolds, Sheldon Danziger, and Harry J. Holzer. 2000. *Detroit Divided.* New York: Russell Sage Foundation.

"Federal Register." 2010. Vol. 75, Pp. 45628–29.

Freeman, Richard B. 1973. "Changes in the Labor Market for Black Americans, 1948–72." *Brookings Papers on Economic Activity* 4(1).

Holzer, Harry J. 2009. "Workforce Development as an Antipoverty Strategy: What Do We Know? What Should We Do?" In *Changing Poverty, Changing Policies*, ed. M. Cancian and S. Danziger (pp. 301–29). New York: Russell Sage Foundation.

Kalousova, L., and S. A. Burgard. 2013. "Debt and Foregone Medical Care." *Journal of Health and Social Behavior* 54(2): 203–19.

Kochhar, Rakesh, Paul Taylor, and Richard Fry. 2011, "Wealth Gaps Rise to Record Highs between Whites, Blacks and Hispanics." Washington, DC: Pew Research Center. Retrieved August 5, 2013, from http://pewsocialtrends.org/files/2011/07/SDT-Wealth-Report_7-26-11_FINAL.pdf.

Mayer, Christopher J., and Karen M. Pence. 2009. "Subprime Mortgage: What, Where, and to Whom?" In *Housing Markets and the Economy*, ed. E. L. Glaeser and J. M. Quigley. Cambridge, MA: Lincoln Institute of Land Policy.

Pettit, Becky. 2012. *Invisible Men: Mass Incarceration and the Myth of Black Progress*. New York: Russell Sage Foundation.

Pfeffer, Fabian T., Sheldon Danziger, and Robert F. Schoeni. 2013. "Wealth Disparities before and after the Great Recession." *Annals of the American Academy of Political and Social Science* 650(1).

Rugh, Jacob S., and Douglas S. Massey. 2010. "Racial Segregation and the American Foreclosure Crisis." *American Sociological Review* 75(5): 629–51.

Shapiro, Thomas, Tatjana Meschede, and Sam Osoro. February 2013. "The Roots of the Widening Racial Wealth Gap: Explaining the Black-White Economic Divide." Waltham, MA: Institute on Assets and Social Policy, Brandeis University.

Chapter Eleven

Integration and Equal Educational Opportunity in the "Post-Racial" Era

Robert A. Sedler

The landmark United States Supreme Court decision in *Brown v. Board of Education* was in retrospect not so much a decision about racial segregation in education as it was a decision about the meaning of racial equality under the Fourteenth Amendment to the Constitution of the United States. While *Brown* itself dealt only with the constitutionality of state-mandated racial segregation in the public schools of seventeen southern and border states, the effect of the Court's holding in that case was to invalidate all state-imposed segregation and with it the official structure of societal racism that existed in the southern part of the nation.

The strategy of the NAACP in attacking state-imposed segregation focused first on the public schools. The theory was that if the Court held unconstitutional state-imposed segregation in the public schools—and the manifest denial of equal educational opportunity for African American children that resulted from state-imposed segregation in the public schools—the rationale of that decision would render unconstitutional all other forms of state-imposed segregation, such as that which existed in transportation and public facilities. The strategy was successful. In a series of brief decisions after *Brown*, the Court invalidated state-imposed segregation in transportation and in all other public facilities. *Brown* was the catalyst for the sweeping movement for civil rights in the years following, and this movement led to the invalidation of all intentional racial discrimination disadvantaging African Americans and other racial minorities and to the enactment of federal and state civil rights laws prohibiting racial discrimination in public accommodations, employment, housing, and voting.

The civil rights movement was followed by affirmative action programs designed to remedy the consequences of a long and tragic history of racial discrimination in this nation and to bring about the full and equal participation of racial minorities in all important areas of American life. While significant disparities between racial minorities and whites unfortunately still remain in terms of income, education, and many other measures of well-being, it cannot be denied that in the half-century after *Brown*, the United States as a nation has moved much closer to achieving a degree of racial equality and that as a nation there is an official commitment to racial equality between minorities and whites.

But the specific holding of *Brown* required a dismantling of the dual school system that existed in the southern and border states, and despite strong and entrenched resistance by those states, by the 1970s, the dual school systems had pretty much been eliminated. At the same time, challenges were being brought to racially discriminatory and segregative practices in school districts outside the south, and these challenges resulted in a number of court orders requiring school desegregation in those districts. The constitutional requirement was that the school districts in constitutional violation achieve the greatest degree of actual desegregation, taking into account the practicalities of the situation, including the often extensive busing of minority children to schools in predominantly white areas and the busing of white children to schools in predominantly minority areas. The result was that there was a good deal of actual desegregation in the southern states and at least some actual desegregation in states outside the south. In a number of school districts in the United States, then, minority children and white children were attending school together, which, as Supreme Court Justice Thurgood Marshall observed, the desegregation of the schools is all about.

However, in the absence of court-ordered desegregation, there is no constitutional requirement that school districts operate racially integrated schools. School districts are organized on a territorial basis, school district by school district. In some states, the county is the basic form of school district organization, but in many states, school districts are organized on a much smaller scale. One of the most enduring consequences of a long history of racial discrimination in this nation, most particularly racial discrimination in the housing delivery system, is residential racial segregation, both within the boundaries of a city or locality and, more significantly, between cities and suburbs. Given the fact that in the nation's major metropolitan areas, the African American and Hispanic population is concentrated in the central cities and the white population is primarily suburban, urban school districts are predominantly African American and Hispanic, and they are surrounded by predominantly white suburban school districts. Since the urban school districts are heavily minority, there is little opportunity for racial integration within the urban school districts.

Conversely, since most suburban school districts are predominantly white, whatever racial integration exists in those school districts is dependent on the number of minority families that have chosen to live in those districts. In addition, even when African American and Hispanic families move to the suburbs, not infrequently, they live in a predominantly minority neighborhood, and once the minority population in a neighborhood reaches a "tipping point," white families tend not to move into those neighborhoods. Finally, most school districts use the geographic attendance area method of school assignment, so that the racial composition of the schools, particularly the elementary schools, will reflect the racial composition of the neighborhood. Stated simply, in the United States today, there is a very high degree of residential racial segregation, and this residential racial segregation is reflected in a large number of racially identifiable schools of one race or another.

Court-ordered desegregation produced racially integrated schools, so long as there were a substantial number of minority children and a substantial number of white students within the school district. However, in many districts, a significant number of white families avoided desegregation by enrolling their children in private schools, and in metropolitan areas, many white families moved out of the urban school district into suburban school districts. And a court-ordered desegregation plan generally was limited to the school district in which the constitutional violation had occurred. So, even when there was a constitutional violation in an urban district such as Detroit, the desegregation plan could not extend to the suburban districts, although at the time the desegregation plan went into effect, the urban district was already heavily African American. It would become even more so, when "white flight" to the suburban school districts reduced the number of white families in the urban school district.

Finally, the Supreme Court held that once a school district had remedied the constitutional violation by eliminating the formerly racially identifiable minority and white schools, the school district had achieved unitary status and so was no longer subject to the desegregation plan. This meant that the school district could, as many chose to do, revert to geographic attendance zoning, which resulted in substantial resegregation and a return to racially identifiable schools. For all of these reasons, the actual desegregation of the public schools, which was significant by the end of the 1980s, began to decline in the 1990s and thereafter, and today, the great majority of African American and Hispanic children, and the great majority of white children, attend racially identifiable schools. At the present time, at least three-quarters of African American children attend schools where more than half the students are minorities, and many of these schools are overwhelmingly minority.

As pointed out previously, the Constitution only prohibits intentional racial segregation in the public schools—that is, segregation required by state law in the seventeen southern and border states, pre-*Brown*, or brought about by intentional segregative acts on the part of school officials, as took place in many districts outside the south in the 1960s and 1970s. There is no constitutional requirement that school districts operate the schools within the district in such a way as to achieve actual desegregation, even where this could be feasibly done, and certainly no constitutional requirement that a state establish a system of school organization that promotes racial integration between predominantly minority urban school districts and predominantly white suburban school districts.

And even though racially discriminatory governmental actions taken in times past significantly contributed to the residential racial segregation and concentration that exists today, this has not been held to impose any constitutional obligation on the states or school districts to try to achieve actual desegregation in the schools. It is for these reasons that from a constitutional standpoint, it is constitutionally permissible to have the situation in the United States today where the great majority of African American and Hispanic students, and the great majority of white students, attend racially identifiable schools.

I now want to turn to the relationship between racial integration and equal educational opportunity, specifically as measured by the academic achievement of African American and Hispanic children. Here we must deal with the overlay of race and social class in American society today. The most significant factor in determining a child's level of academic achievement, as measured by standardized academic achievement tests, is the social-class background of the child. Children coming from economically advantaged backgrounds in the aggregate will have substantially higher levels of academic achievement than children coming from economically disadvantaged backgrounds.

This is so obvious as to need no explanation or demonstration. But the second most important factor and the major school factor in determining a child's level of academic achievement is the social-class composition of the child's classroom. Classrooms in which economically advantaged children predominate will in the aggregate have higher levels of academic achievement than classrooms in which economically disadvantaged children predominate, and this includes the economically disadvantaged children enrolled in such classrooms. That is, the level of academic achievement of economically disadvantaged children enrolled in classes in which economically advantaged children predominate will in the aggregate be higher than it would have been if the same children were enrolled in classrooms in which economically disadvantaged predominate, although in the aggregate, it will not be as high as the level of the economically advantaged children. Stated simply, the best way to improve the academic achievement of economically disadvantaged children is to enroll them in classrooms in which economically advantaged children predominate.

And since the predominant class composition of the classroom will be economically advantaged children, this can be accomplished without any diminution in the academic achievement of the economically advantaged children. A classroom in which say, 75 percent of the children are economically advantaged will produce the same level of academic achievement for the economically advantaged children as a classroom in which 100 percent of the children are economically advantaged—although many parents of economically advantaged children don't believe this. But both points are true, and they have been empirically demonstrated by numerous academic studies over a long period of time.

The correlation between racial integration and the improved academic achievement of minority students results not from racial integration, but from social-class integration. In a system-wide desegregation program, such as the court-ordered desegregation of the Louisville-Jefferson County, Kentucky, schools, the desegregation was between the predominantly white and middle-class suburban part of Jefferson County and the predominantly African American and lower-income City of Louisville. I was the lead counsel for the plaintiffs in that case in the 1970s, when I was teaching at the University of Kentucky. When the desegregation plan—which included the required merger of the formerly separate Louisville and Jefferson County school systems—went into effect in the fall, 1975, the merged system was approximately 80 percent white and 20 percent African American. The elementary schools were integrated at between 12 and 44 percent African American students, and the secondary schools were integrated at between 14 and 24 percent African American students.

This meant that all of the schools were majority white schools, and with few, if any, exceptions, they were predominantly middle-class schools. We predicted that this would produce academic benefits for the predominantly economically disadvantaged African American children, since they would be enrolled in classrooms in which economically advantaged white students predominated. In addition, now that the schools were integrated, there would necessarily be a sharing of educational resources between African American and white children in all of the schools.

The plaintiffs in this action were predominantly lower- and moderate-income African American parents of children enrolled in the Louisville schools. They desperately wanted their children to attend integrated schools, and when there was substantial opposition to the desegregation plan by white parents, including a boycott of the schools, and members of the Kentucky National Guard were "riding shotgun" on the school buses, the African American children were standing on the street corner waiting for the buses to transport them to the formerly white—and not always hospitable—schools in Jefferson County.

They were not seeking integration for integration's sake, or for the considerable intangible benefits to children that come from attendance at racially integrated schools. They wanted a good education for their children, and they knew that if they children were able to attend racially integrated schools, it is likely that they would get a much better education and have higher levels of academic achievement than they would have had if the children had been attending racially identifiable African American schools. In the final analysis, schools in which white children predominate are in fact generally academically superior to schools in which African American children predominate, and the plaintiffs in this action knew it. In the "real world," as a large number of academic studies demonstrate, African American children attending racially integrated schools—for the most part schools that were racially integrated under court order—will in the aggregate have higher levels of academic achievement than African American children attending predominantly African American schools. It is not a matter of race, but of the social-class composition of the classroom and the availability of the same educational resources that are available to the white children.

This is what happened in Louisville-Jefferson County. In fact, not only did the academic achievement scores of the African American children improve in the years following implementation of the desegregation program, but the academic achievement scores of both African American and white students improved in relation to national norms. And, despite initial intense opposition to the desegregation plan, public attitudes changed, and the Jefferson County Board of Education made a policy decision to continue the racial integration program, even after it was no longer subject to the court-ordered desegregation decree.

The program was modified after the Supreme Court in 2007 imposed some limits on voluntary integration programs, including a ban on assigning individual students to schools on the basis of race. The modified plan takes into account socioeconomic factors such as income and educational levels of the neighborhood as well as race, and provides a degree of parental choice. The modified plan ensures that there will continue to be substantial racial and socioeconomic integration in the Jefferson County schools today.

The point to be emphasized here is that totally apart from what may be called the social and educational advantages of a diverse student body, attendance at racially integrated schools will in the aggregate result in improved educational opportunities and higher levels of academic achievement for African American and Hispanic children. That this improved educational opportunity for African American and Hispanic children may not be due to race is irrelevant. The improved educational opportunity is there, and a decline in the number of African American and Hispanic children attending racially integrated schools has resulted in a diminution in equal educational opportunity for many African American and Hispanic children today.

The reality today then, as we have said, is that the great majority of African American and Hispanic children attend racially identifiable schools. And by far the largest number of them attend school in large urban school districts such as Detroit, Chicago, and Philadelphia, where the school population is overwhelmingly minority and predominantly lower income. It is at this point that the objective of racial integration in the schools must take account of race and social class. Middle-class African American and Hispanic families can choose good-quality, racially integrated public schools for their children by moving to the suburban school districts that surround predominantly minority and lower-income urban school districts.

The same may be true for "working-class" African American and Hispanic families where there are good public schools in the "working-class" suburbs in the metropolitan area. Or middle-class African American and Hispanic parents, like middle-class white parents, can choose private schools for their children. Today, then, the children of middle-class African American and Hispanic families will have all the educational advantages that middle-class family background brings.

They will have equal educational opportunity with the middle-class white children enrolled in suburban and private schools, and it is these African American and Hispanic children that are sought out by universities across the nation that are seeking to enroll a diverse student body.

So, when we talk about equal educational opportunity for African American and Hispanic children today, we have moved from race to social class. We are talking about the predominantly lower-income African American and Hispanic children that are enrolled in the large and heavily minority and lower-income urban school districts in the nation's major metropolitan areas.

We are not now talking about integration as a means of providing equal educational opportunity for these children, because there are not very many white students enrolled in the large urban school districts, and the white students enrolled there are predominantly lower income as well. We will see racial integration in suburban school districts into which significant numbers of middle-class African American and Hispanic families have moved and perhaps in some "blue-collar" school districts, such as those that exist in suburban Detroit, that have good-quality public schools. We will see racial integration in large countywide districts or urban districts such as Louisville-Jefferson County, Kentucky, that have substantial minority and white populations and that have made affirmative efforts to achieve racially integrated schools within the district. But, as we have said, only a limited number of African American and Hispanic children will be enrolled in racially integrated schools.

Since the overwhelming number of African American and Hispanic children are enrolled in large and heavily minority and predominantly lower-income large urban school districts, the objective of achieving equal educational opportunity—or perhaps more accurately, improved educational opportunity—for these children must focus on substantially improving the quality of education now provided by the large urban school districts in which these children are enrolled. "Race to the Top" and similar programs are directed toward achieving this objective. Hopefully, they will be successful, and in the years ahead, we will see improved educational opportunity and improved levels of academic achievement for these African American and Hispanic children. But we can no longer rely on racial integration to achieve this objective.

Chapter Twelve

Conclusion

Integration Resources

Curtis L. Ivery and Joshua A. Bassett

The challenge to reclaim the project of integration in American society is arguably today as significant as it was in the 1960s during the Kennedy/Johnson administrations and the advent of civil rebellions that swept across urban centers throughout the United States. These rebellions, which have been importantly analyzed in areas of scholarship concerning America's "urban crisis, " were driven by preceding decades of legal segregation in education, housing, economics, and political spheres with enduring impacts that still operate in the present day, but in a new social-discursive context based on fallacious ideas that race/racial identity no longer functions as a barrier to opportunity in the U.S. and that we have a become a color-blind and post-racial society. The various essays in this collection, as well as an enormous amount of scholarship in a diverse range of academic fields, definitively proves this thesis otherwise by identifying the continuing salience of the relationship between race and inequality, yet despite this substantial work the efforts to address these issues on a national scale remain scarce, with an even more hostile resistance to implementing actual structural policies that could abate these inequalities.

The purpose of this collection is to provide a wider understanding of how race/racial identity continues to influence key areas of American life and to also help to develop a framework by which communities in a wide spectrum of fields (e.g., education, politics, law, neighborhood organizations, media, etc.) can more effectively respond to the impacts of racial inequalities that continue to divide our nation and obstruct our progress to achieving a truly democratic state. In our view, and especially in the predominant context of color-blind and post-racial discourse, the project of voluntary racial integration remains the determinative solution for advancing the interests of American democracy, and specifically so, as the nation continues its unprecedented transformation into a multiracial majority.

There are indeed viable approaches to be availed to reclaim integration. Broadly, as numerous scholars have noted, this would involve a renewed effort via the U.S. Department of Education to shift its emphasis on "high-stakes" testing and its promotion of "market-place" schooling to a focus on the need to promote educational equity through voluntary forms of integration, which would also directly include strong collaborations between institutions of higher education and K-12 systems. Similar work via institutions/arenas of law dealing with "disparate impacts" of enduring racial segregation and discrimination in housing and related areas (banking, loans, other forms of capital, etc.) is also crucial to these efforts as this directly affects access to schooling and a wide spectrum of economic and political outcomes. These are but two critical areas where reclaiming the project of integration would have a beneficial impact and there are certainly numerous others, but as the title of this collection identifies, reclaiming the language of race from its now dominant constructions within post-racial discourse and as propagated through majority forms of media is also critical to this project.

We offer here, in this brief conclusion, a partial list of integration resources, with a particular recognition of the decades of work of Gary Orfield and his colleagues at the Civil Rights Project/Proyecto Derechos at UCLA (and preceding work at the Harvard Civil Project), including specific policy, legislative, and educational/research resources that can be applied to pursue voluntary forms of integration and racial equity in educational, legal, and institutional capacities:

1. Civil Rights Project/Proyecto Derechos Civiles at UCLA: This is arguably the most influential university-based institute of its kind providing resources and support for integration of U.S. schools.
2. The National Coalition on School Diversity: Members include leading legal, educational, and civil rights entities working on issues/areas of integration and equity.
3. Haas Institute for a Fair and Inclusive Society: Leading multidisciplinary national university-based institute focusing on diversity, equity, and social inclusion.
4. Charles Hamilton Houston Institute for Race and Justice at Harvard Law School: Leading institute in legal areas of civil rights, integration, racial equity.
5. University of North Carolina Center for Civil Rights: Leading legal and civil rights center focusing on issues of equity and social justice, especially in the Southern United States.

6. The Campaign for Educational Equity, Teachers College Columbia: Leading institute focusing on key issues of educational equity.
7. The National Center for Institutional Diversity (NCID): Located at the University of Michigan, NCID focuses on critical issues of diversity in higher education.
8. American Association of Community Colleges (AACC): Primary advocacy entity of community colleges, the AACC features many community college members that offer high school dual enrollment programs that can be critical in promoting voluntary integration in education.
9. Oak Park Regional Housing Center (Oak Park, Illinois): Executive director Rob Breymaier helms one of the oldest and most influential centers of its kind in the nation in promoting integration and sustainable diversity in residential neighborhoods.

The Democracy Commitment Project: National collective of community colleges focusing on democratic inclusion and equity.

Index

About the Contributors

Dr. Curtis L. Ivery is a nationally renowned leader in U.S. urban affairs. He is the author of numerous books on urban issues and was the first African-American appointed by President Bill Clinton to the Governor's Cabinet in the state of Arkansas as the Commissioner for the Department of Health and Human Services. He has written extensively for newspapers and magazines and has conceived several nationally acclaimed conferences focusing on key issues of urban inequality and social justice. This is the second and completing volume to his past work, *America's Urban Crisis and the Advent of Color-blind Politics* (Rowman & Littlefield, 2011).

Joshua A. Bassett is Director of the Institute for Social Progress (ISP), a nationally affiliated urban studies and educational institute located at Wayne County Community College District in Detroit, Michigan. He served as executive director of the "Educational Summit: Detroit and the Crisis in Urban America Conference" (broadcast nationally on C-Span network). His past work includes *America's Urban Crisis and the Advent of Color-blind Politics: Education, Incarceration, Segregation and the Future of U.S. Multiracial Democracy,* (Rowman & Littlefield, 2011).

Sheldon H. Danziger is the president of the Russell Sage Foundation. Previously he was the Henry J. Meyer Distinguished University Professor of Public Policy at the Gerald R. Ford School of Public Policy, research professor at the Population Studies Center, and director of the National Poverty Center at the University of Michigan. He is a member of the American Academy of Arts and Sciences and a John Kenneth Galbraith Fellow of the American Academy of Political and Social Science, and he has been a John Simon Guggenheim Foundation Fellow and a visiting scholar at the Russell Sage Foundation and at the Rockefeller Foundation's Bellagio Center. Between 1989 and 2013, Danziger directed the Research and Training Program on Poverty and Public Policy at the University of Michigan, a training and mentorship program for developing the careers of emerging scholars from underrepresented groups.

Three of Danziger's books have been selected as Noteworthy Books in Industrial Relations and Labor Economics by Princeton University's Industrial Relations Section: The Price of Independence: The Economics of Early Adulthood (co-edited with Cecilia Rouse, Russell Sage Foundation, 2007); Working and Poor: How Economic Conditions and Policy Changes Affect Low-Wage Workers (co-edited with Rebecca Blank and Robert Schoeni, Russell Sage Foundation, 2006); and America Unequal, co-authored with Peter Gottschalk (Harvard University Press and Russell Sage Foundation, 1995). Other books include Detroit Divided, co-authored with Reynolds Farley and Harry Holzer (Russell Sage Foundation, 2000), Changing Poverty, Changing Policies (co-edited with Maria Cancian, Russell Sage Foundation, 2009) and Legacies of the War on Poverty (co-edited with Martha Bailey, Russell Sage Foundation, 2013).

Reynolds Farley is a research scientist at the Population Studies Center in the Institute for Social Research and the Otis Dudley Duncan Professor Emeritus at the University of Michigan. His research focuses upon current population trends in the United States with an emphasis upon racial differences. He participated in the 1980, 1990, and 2000 census research series sponsored by the Russell Sage Foundation and directed the University of Michigan's Detroit Area Study three times. He has written extensively about racial and economic trends in the Detroit area and now maintains a website, www.Detroit1701. org describing the history and future of that dynamic metropolis. He teaches short courses at the Gerald Ford School of Public Policy concerning Detroit and has prepared several reports about recent trends in Michigan. Reynolds Farley earned his doctoral degree at the University of Chicago and taught at Duke University before coming to the University of Michigan in 1967.

Erica Frankenberg is an assistant professor in the Department of Education Policy Studies in the College of Education at The Pennsylvania State University. Current research projects include studying suburban racial change, policy and politics of responses to the Supreme Court's decision about voluntary integration, and how school choice policies affect racial stratification. She has coauthored or coedited several recent books including *Educational Delusions? Why Choice Can Deepen Inequality and How to Make It Fair* (with Gary Orfield), *The Resegregation of Suburban Schools: A Hidden Crisis in American Education* (with Gary Orfield), and *Integrating Schools in a*

Changing Society (with Elizabeth DeBray). Additionally, she has served as coeditor of a special issue of the *Peabody Journal of Education*. Her work has been published in education policy journals, law reviews, and practitioner publications. Prior to coming to Penn State, she was a research and policy associate at the Civil Rights Project. She received her doctorate in educational policy from Harvard University and undergraduate degree from Dartmouth College. She is a native of Mobile, Alabama, where she attended desegregated schools. Frankenberg has also assisted several districts with the design of their diversity policy and has served as an expert witness in several school diversity cases.

Eddie Glaude Jr., PhD, Princeton University, is the William S. Tod Professor of Religion and African American Studies, Department of Religion, and chair of the Center for African American Studies. Professor Glaude's research interests include American pragmatism, specifically the work of John Dewey, and African American religious history and its place in American public life. He is the recipient of numerous fellowships and awards, including the 2002 Modern Language Association William Sanders Scarborough Prize for his book *Exodus!*

Lucie Kalousova is a doctoral candidate in sociology and health policy and a trainee in population studies at the University of Michigan. Her research addresses the mechanisms through which social inequality translates to health disparities both in the United States and in Europe. She has been analyzing the Michigan Recession and Recovery Study survey data to understand the effects of the Great Recession on health and well-being of the Southeast Michigan residents. Her work on this topic has been published by the *Annual Review of Sociology*, *Journal of Health and Social Behavior*, and *Social Science and Medicine*, among others.

Maria Krysan is professor in the Department of Sociology and the Institute of Government and Public Affairs at the University of Illinois at Chicago. Her research interests are racial residential segregation, racial attitudes, and survey methodology.

Gary Orfield is distinguished research professor of education, law, political science and urban planning at UCLA and professor emeritus of education and social policy at Harvard University. Orfield is a political scientist and leading scholar in the study of civil rights, education policy, urban policy, and minority opportunity. He was cofounder and director of the Civil Rights Project at Harvard, an initiative that developed and published a new generation of research on multiracial civil rights issues. The project relocated in 2007 to UCLA, where it was renamed the Civil Rights Project/Proyecto Derechos Civiles and is currently codirected by Orfield and Patricia Gándara. Orfield's central interest has been the development and implementation of social policy, with a central focus on the impact of policy on equal opportunity for success in American society. Works since 2000 include eleven authored or edited books (many with coauthors) and numerous articles and reports. In addition to his scholarly work, Orfield has been involved with development of governmental policy and has served as an expert witness or special master in several dozen class action civil rights cases related to his research, including the University of Michigan Supreme Court case that upheld the policy of affirmative action in 2003. He has been called to give testimony in civil rights suits by the United States Department of Justice and many civil rights, legal services, and educational organizations. In 2006, 2012, and 2013, he and colleagues wrote amicus briefs, signed by hundreds of scholars across the United States and submitted to the Supreme Court, summarizing research on issues of school desegregation and affirmative action in higher education. *Diversity Challenged*, his book with M. Kurlaender, was cited by the Supreme Court in the 2003 *Grutter* decision upholding affirmative action. He was also awarded the American Political Science Association's Charles Merriam Award for "contribution to the art of government through the application of social science research," and the 2007 Social Justice award of the American Education Research Association for work having "a profound impact in demonstrating the critical role of education research in supporting social justice." He is a member of the National Academy of Education and received honorary doctorates from Wheelock College and Pennsylvania State University. As the director and codirector of the Civil Rights Project, he has commissioned and edited hundreds of original studies of civil rights issues, organized many national conferences, and lectured widely at leading U.S. universities and other settings, and in several European and Latin American nations, China, and South Africa. A native Minnesotan, Orfield received his BA summa cum laude from the University of Minnesota, MA and PhD from the University of Chicago, and lives and works part of each year in the Centro Histórico of Mexico City. Orfield is married to Patricia Gándara, and has three daughters and seven grandchildren.

Professor **john a. powell** is executive director of the Haas Institute for a Fair and Inclusive Society (HIFIS) and Robert D. Haas Chancellor's Chair in Equity and Inclusion at the University of California, Berkeley. Formerly, he directed the Kirwan Institute for the Study of Race and Ethnicity at The Ohio State University and the Institute for Race and Poverty at the University of Minnesota. He led the development of an "opportunity-based" model that connects affordable housing to racialized spaces in education, health, health care, and employment. He is the author of *Racing to Justice: Transforming our Concepts of Self and Other to Build an Inclusive Society*. The author does not capitalize his name.

Robert A. Sedler is Distinguished Professor of Law at Wayne State University in Detroit, where he teaches the courses in constitutional law and conflict of laws. Prior to coming to Wayne State in 1977, he was professor of law at the University of Kentucky. Professor Sedler is a graduate of the University of Pittsburgh and its school of law. From 2000 to 2005, he held the Gibbs Chair in Civil Rights and Civil Liberties. In 2005, he was elected to the Wayne State University Academy of Scholars, and served as its president during the 2007–2008 academic year. Professor Sedler has published extensively in both of his fields, and there have been many citations to his works by courts and academic commentators. He is also the author of *Constitutional Law in the United States* (2nd ed. 2014). Professor Sedler has litigated a large number of civil rights and civil liberties cases in Michigan, Kentucky, and elsewhere, mostly as a volunteer lawyer for the American Civil Liberties Union. While in Kentucky, he was the lead counsel in two cases that desegregated the Louisville-Jefferson County public schools and the Lexington-Fayette County public schools. He has received numerous awards for his work in civil rights and civil liberties.

Andrew Grant Thomas is director of programs at Proteus Fund, a grant-making organization whose donor collaboratives strategically direct funding toward grassroots initiatives focused on money in politics, marriage equality, abolition of the death penalty, and protection of civil liberties in the post-9/11 national security environment. His expertise includes structural opportunity and systems thinking, racial equity, poverty alleviation, implicit bias and racial communications, and multiracial alliance building.

Before joining Proteus in 2012, Andrew was deputy director of the Kirwan Institute for the Study of Race and Ethnicity at the Ohio State University, overseeing much of the Institute's programming while serving as editor-in-chief of its Race/Ethnicity journal and director of its biennial Transforming Race conference. Prior to that work Andrew was with the Civil Rights Project at Harvard University. He earned his bachelor's degree in literature from Yale University, and his master's in international relations and PhD in political science from the University of Chicago.

Howard Winant is professor of sociology at the University of California, Santa Barbara, where he is also affiliated with the Black Studies, Chicana/o

Studies, and Asian American Studies departments. He received his PhD from the University of California, Santa Cruz in 1980. Winant has worked and taught in Mexico, Brazil, and Argentina.

Winant is the founding director of the University of California Center for New Racial Studies (UCCNRS), a MultiCampus Research Program Initiative. He is the author of *Racial Formation in the United States* (2014, 1994, 1986; coauthor, Michael Omi); *The New Politics of Race: Globalism, Difference, Justice* (2004); *The World Is a Ghetto: Race and Democracy since World War II* (2001); *Racial Conditions: Politics, Theory, Comparisons* (1994); and *Stalemate: Political Economic Origins of Supply-Side Policy* (1988).